More Brainstorms

Also by Don Rubin

WHAT'S THE BIG IDEA?
THOSE INCREDIBLE PUZZLES
THINK TANK
REAL PUZZLE BOOK #1
REAL PUZZLE BOOK #2
REAL PUZZLE BOOK #3
BRAINSTORMS

More Brainstorms

Real Puzzles for the Real Genius

by Don Rubin

with illustrations by Roger Jones

HarperPerennial
A Division of HarperCollinsPublishers

FIRST EDITION

ISBN 0-06-096829-X

90 91 92 93 94 MPC 10 9 8 7 6 5 4 3 2 1

Contents

More Brainstorms

1. Shake-up

Jackie meet Chris. Tracy meet Sandy. Sandy meet Dale. Dale meet Chris. Chris meet Sandy. Jackie meet Pat.

Using the introductions above as a guide, you should be able to identify each of the numbered pairs of hands at the right.

1) —————————————

2) —————————————

3) —————————————

4) —————————————

5) —————————————

6) —————————————

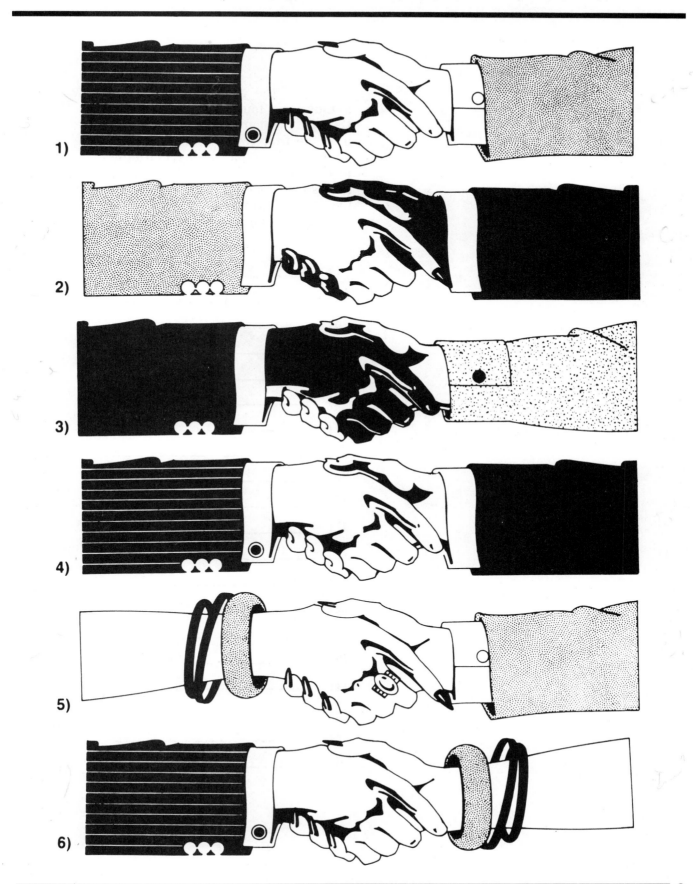

1)

2)

3)

4)

5)

6)

2. Four-letter words

Each of the graphics at the right stands for a four-letter word. In fact, the last two letters of each word are also the first two letters of the next word. (For example, the last two letters in the word "hobo" are the first two letters in the word "bone," whose last two letters begin "nest.")

See if you can identify all the words.

1) _____

2) _____

3) _____

4) _____

5) _____

6) _____

7) _____

8) _____

9) _____

10) _____

11) _____

12) _____

13) _____

14) _____

15) _____

16) _____

17) _____

18) _____

19) _____

20) _____

1

2

3

4

5

6

7

8

9

10

11

12

13

14

15

16

17

18

19

20

3. Mental blocks

Which of these lettered patterns form cubes when folded along the dotted lines?

Remember, these are *mental* blocks, so try not to cut them out. The object of the exercise is to determine the box score in your head. Then indicate the answers below.

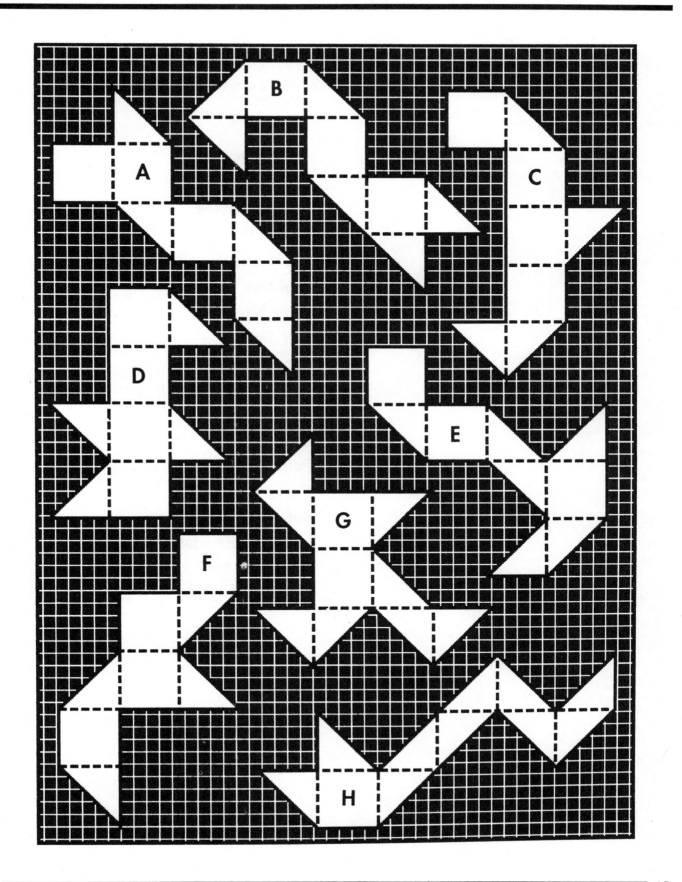

4. War games

See if you can match the ribbons at the right with the battles, wars, conflicts, etc., listed below.

___ **British Invasion**

___ **Custody Battle**

___ **Big Mac Attack**

___ **War on Poverty**

___ **Heart Attack**

___ **Cold War**

___ **Price Wars**

___ **Star Wars**

___ **Armageddon**

___ **Battle of the Sexes**

___ **Media Blitz**

___ **Saturday Night Massacre**

___ **Political Campaign**

___ **War of the Worlds**

___ **Battle of Wits**

___ **Industrial Revolution**

___ **Invasion of the Body Snatchers**

___ **Sexual Revolution**

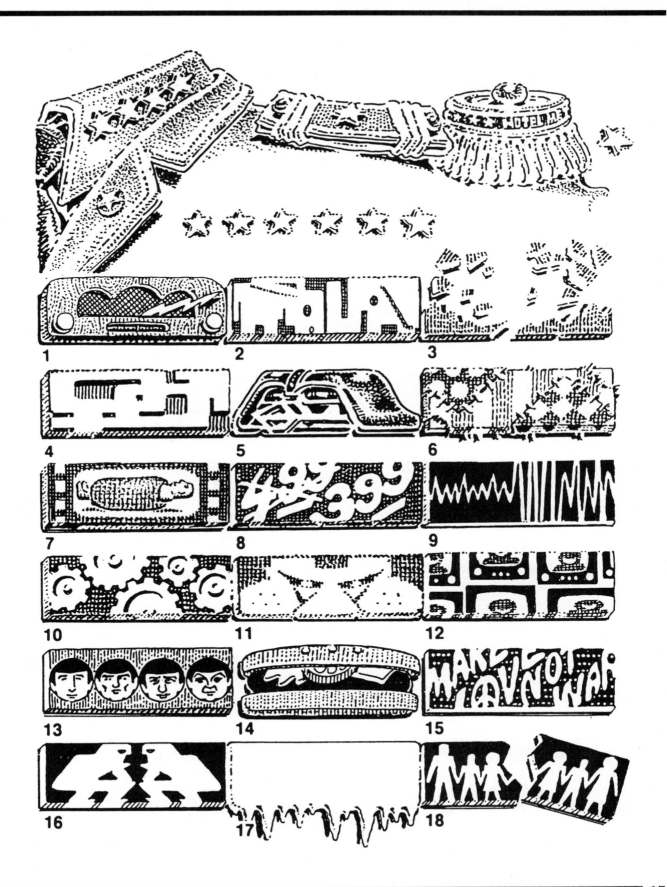

1

2

3

4

5

6

7

8

9

10

11

12

13

14

15

16

17

18

5. Fare game

Maple syrup comes from Vermont, which means that item 1 probably should have been set in the rustic typeface that looks like tree limbs (item 6). Of course that means you'll have to change "chow mein" too, and all the rest of the fare.

Fill in the blanks below.

1) ___**6**___
2) _____
3) _____
4) _____
5) _____
6) _____
7) _____
8) _____
9) _____
10) _____
11) _____
12) _____

1. MAPLE SYRUP
2. SALISBURY STEAK
3. POPCORN
4. MOUSSAKA
5. CHILI CON CARNE
6. CHOW MEIN
7. SAUERKRAUT
8. KNISHES
9. VINDALOO
10. TANG
11. borscht
12. Baba Ganoosh

6. Odd ball

We've combined segments from 16 spherical objects at the right and scrambled their names below. Have a ball.

1) BLYEAEL

2) BDERLIAROMLR

3) ALBOFLGL

4) ARGONE

5) FLBLILHEFAW

6) ANBLINLTSE

7) LOAFNBRLAY

8) ABLIBLIDALRL

9) RUBEYEBRL

10) THEREHAT

11) LEASTABLKB

12) THENANTRSORSMMACI

13) LACBLORCSE

14) ERCCEPTTNEO

15) BELSLABA

16) ONEMHTO

7. Lost and found

Amelia Earhart was headed for this remote speck of land on July 2, 1937, when her Lockheed Electra 10-E vanished. Her mysterious disappearance marked the end of her famous attempt to circumnavigate the globe by the longest and most hazardous route, along the equator.

Earhart (and navigator Fred Noonan) never found the airstrip built especially for her. Can you? Name the island.

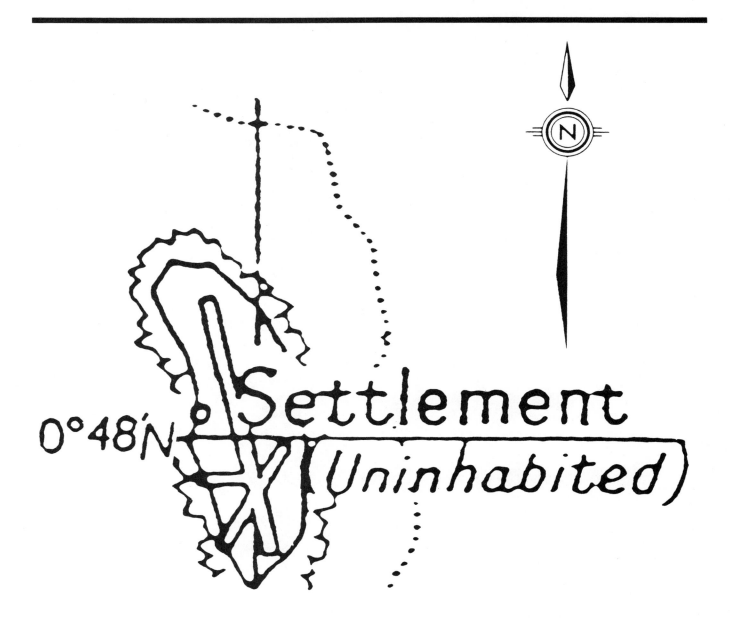

0°48′N

Settlement
(Uninhabited)

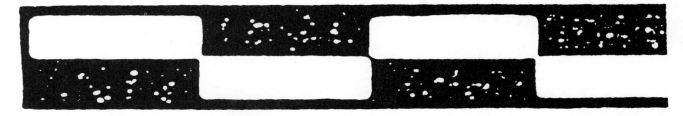

scale

8. Paint can

There's a Universal Product Code on nearly everything these days. To solve this puzzle you'll have to do a little comparison shopping.

Compare the codes you find around the house with the code at the right. Then jot the correct numerical subtitle (10 digits) in the spaces below the bars.

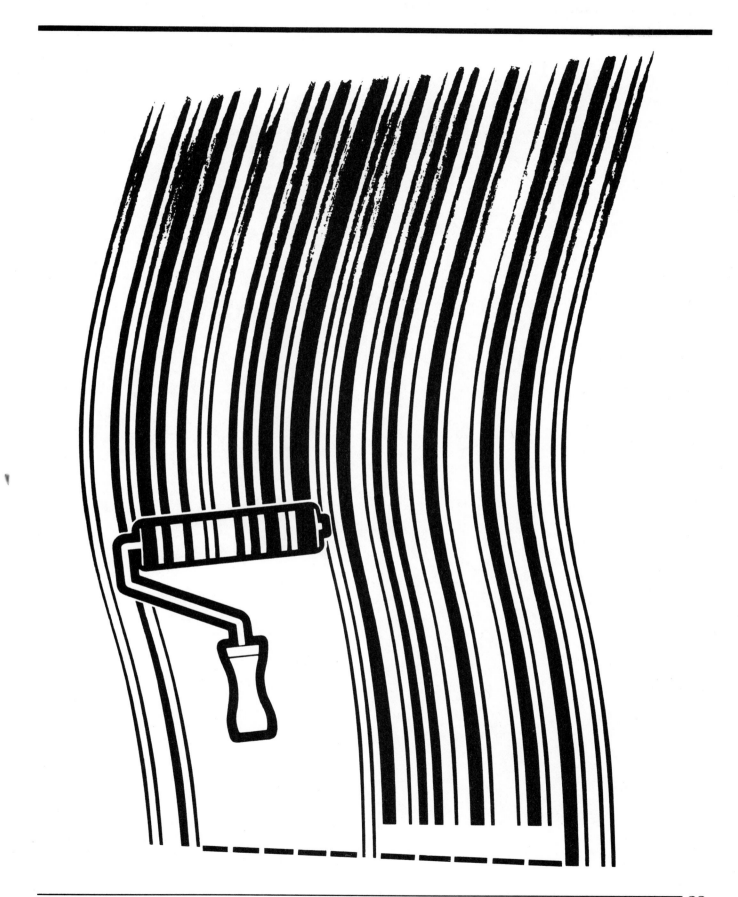

9. Package deal

Each of the scenes at the right depicts a moment in a woman's shopping trip. Using the various clues, see if you can number the panels chronologically.

10. With E's

Each of the typefaces at the right has a name that more or less describes it. See how many you can identify.

___ American Typewriter

_11_ Neon

___ Ivy League

___ Old English

___ Stack

___ Brush Script

___ Domino

___ L.C.D.

___ Scimitar

___ Croissant

___ Stencil

___ Television

___ Masquerade

___ Rush

___ Ringlet

___ Pin Ball

___ Sampler

___ Rope

___ Fleurdon

___ Smile

___ Data

___ Xerxes

___ Rickshaw

___ Marquee

___ Lariat

___ Quicksilver

___ Shatter

___ Rustic

_7_ Chromium One

___ Fingers

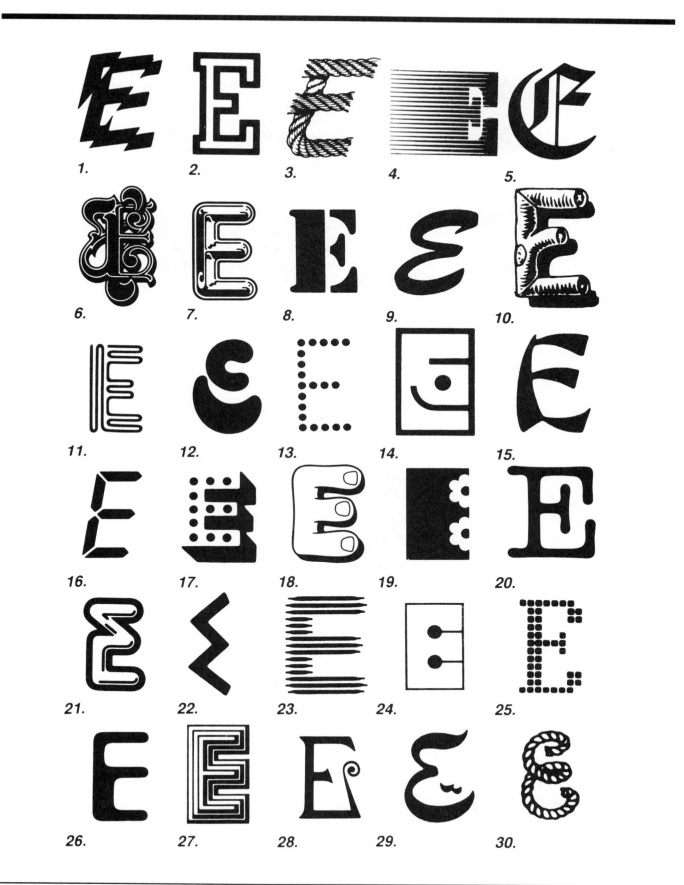

1. 2. 3. 4. 5.

6. 7. 8. 9. 10.

11. 12. 13. 14. 15.

16. 17. 18. 19. 20.

21. 22. 23. 24. 25.

26. 27. 28. 29. 30.

11. Marquee de Sade

Theater owners could save a fortune in giant plastic letters if they just ran movies with overlapping titles. *Purple Rain Man of La Mancha*, for example, saves seven letters.

Of course, the first and last words *(Purple La Mancha)* are all that any *real* film buff would need to figure out the rest.

We've given you the opening and closing words of 25 triple features. See if you can name the movies.

MARQUEE

PURPLE RAIN MAN
OF LA MANCHA
PRINCE HOFFMAN O'TOOLE

1) Melvin _____ Soup
2) Sleeping _____ Fathoms
3) King _____ Story
4) Dirty _____ Passage
5) Dr. _____ Africa
6) Watership _____ Cop
7) Starting _____ Gun
8) ...And _____ Town
9) A Patch _____ Wish
10) The Big _____ West
11) The Blackboard _____ American
12) Bronco _____ Galahad
13) Blume _____ Mercies
14) Trading _____ Hunter
15) April _____ Bullet
16) Anne _____ Wait
17) Who _____ Deep
18) ...And _____ Dangerously
19) Dinner _____ Hard
20) Bright _____ Love
21) Talk _____ Roses
22) Fool _____ 2000
23) They _____ Bingo
24) Anatomy _____ Nile
25) The Elephant _____ 13th

12. See shells?

See if you can unscramble the shells'
names below.

1) AZLMARCRO

_____

2) KEEPINLWIR

_____

3) OUHGQA

_____

4) NHCCO

_____

5) SADRONALDL

_____

6) YESROT

_____

7) CLEANBAR

_____

8) WYORC

_____

9) BEANLOA

_____

10) LOCALSP

_____

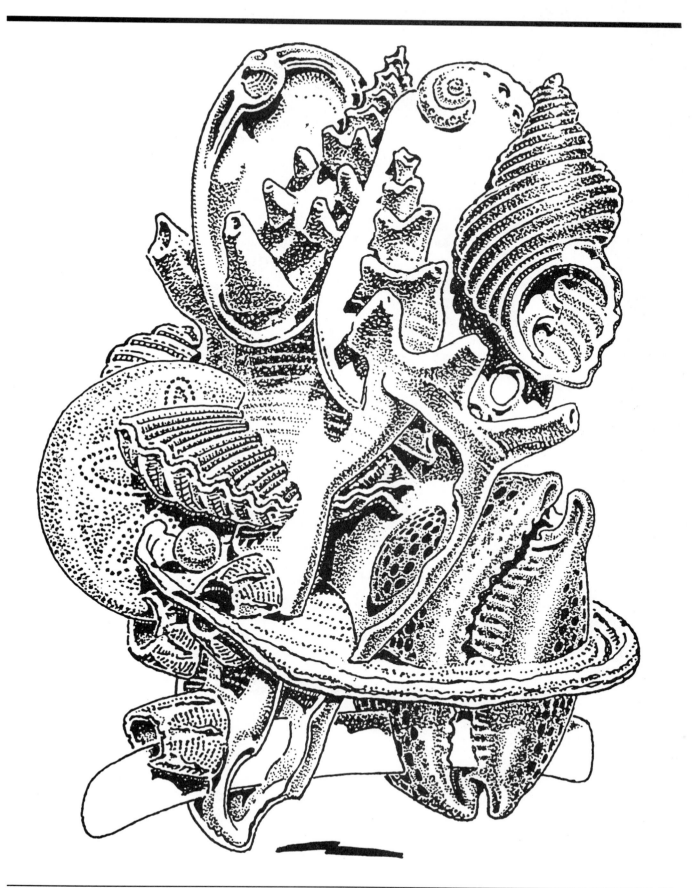

13. Jigsquare

Cut out the puzzle pieces and put them together—you're halfway there. Your finished jigsaw will be a portrait of a famous person. Who?

_____

14. Blots

Ruth Stuart and Albert Paine created these inkblots (which they called "Gobolinks") in 1896, more than 20 years before Rorschach introduced his famous test. They gave the blots names, which we've listed below. See if you can match them up.

__9__ The Friendly Chickens

___ The Butterfly

___ Fishing for Shadow-Fish

__6__ A South Sea Idol

___ The Butterfly Man

___ The Grenadier

___ A Fanciful Elk

__12__ Miss F.M. De Lisle

__14__ A Glad Return

___ The Cathode (X-ray)

___ Queen Beetle

__5__ King Beetle

___ Good Breeding

___ The Washerwomen

___ The Mirror

___ Our Pet

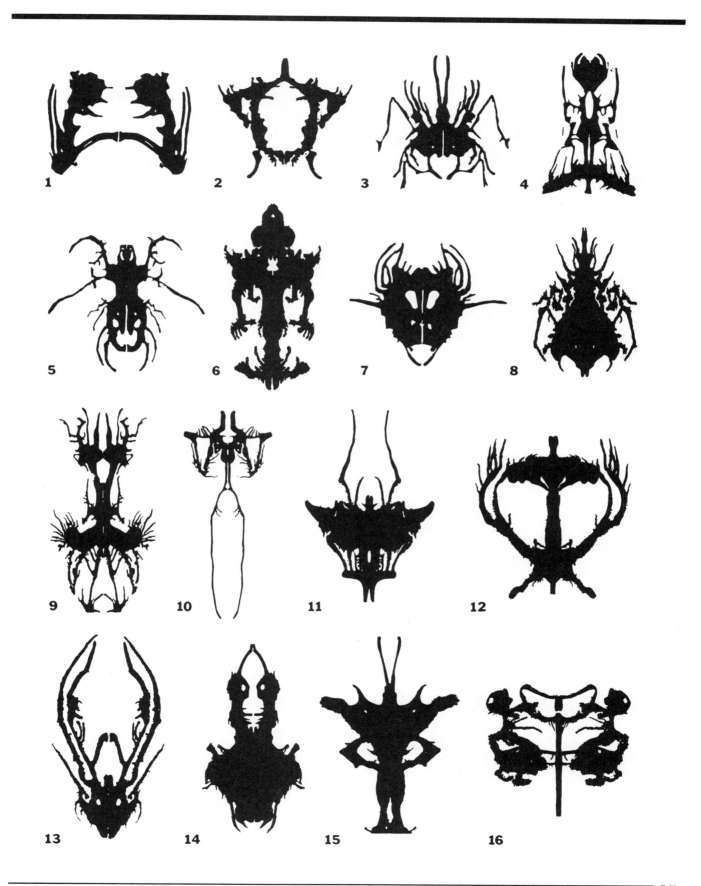

15. Final round

Today's Final Jeopardy category is "Game Shows." You know how this works. Fill in your answer below.

_____

_____

THIS SUM
IS THE
LARGEST DOLLAR
AMOUNT
A CONTESTANT CAN WIN
IN A STANDARD GAME
OF
JEOPARDY!

16. Cereal killer

We've removed the names from the 16 cereal boxes at the right and listed them below. Match the names and boxes.

___ **ALPHA-BITS**

___ **CORN POPS**

___ **CRISPIX**

___ **RICE KRISPIES**

___ **CORN FLAKES**

___ **MUESLIX**

___ **HONEY SMACKS**

___ **FROOT LOOPS**

___ **GRAPE-NUTS**

___ **FROSTED MINI-WHEATS**

___ **RAISIN BRAN**

___ **PRODUCT 19**

___ **NUT & HONEY CRUNCH**

___ **FROSTED FLAKES**

___ **ALL-BRAN**

___ **SPECIAL K**

17. Vase to vase

Each of the numbered vases at the right contains the profiles of two lettered characters listed below.

a) Jay Leno
b) Michael Dukakis
c) Ronald Reagan
d) Fidel Castro
e) Henry Kissinger
f) Mikhail Gorbachev
g) Groucho Marx
h) Charlton Heston
i) Abraham Lincoln
j) Spencer Tracy
k) Fearless Fosdick
l) Bob Dylan
m) Marlon Brando
n) Katharine Hepburn
o) Chico Marx
p) Ingrid Bergman
q) Playboy
r) Woody Allen
s) Uncle Sam
t) Dick Tracy
u) Elvis Presley
v) The New Yorker
w) George Bush
x) Humphrey Bogart

See if you can match them up, as shown.

1) u - l   2) — · —   3) — · —
4) — · —   5) — · —   6) — · —
7) — · —   8) — · —   9) — · —
10) — · —   11) — · —   12) — · —

18. Oversight

Each of the strikeovers at the right is actually a pair of related characters whose names are typed one on top of the other. Can you identify them?

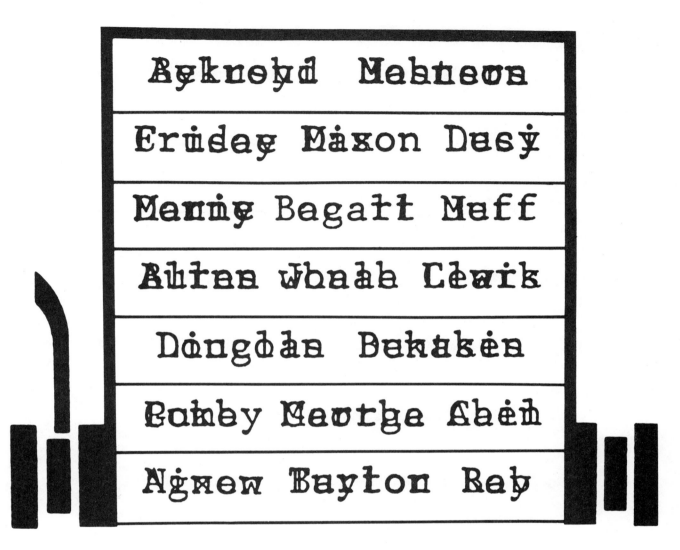

19. Dead letters

We'd like you to identify the characters whose initials appear on these imaginary memorial stones. Okay, gang, letter RIP.

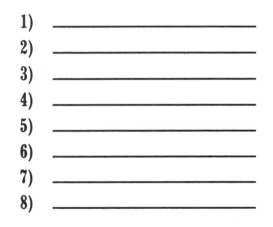

1) _____

2) _____

3) _____

4) _____

5) _____

6) _____

7) _____

8) _____

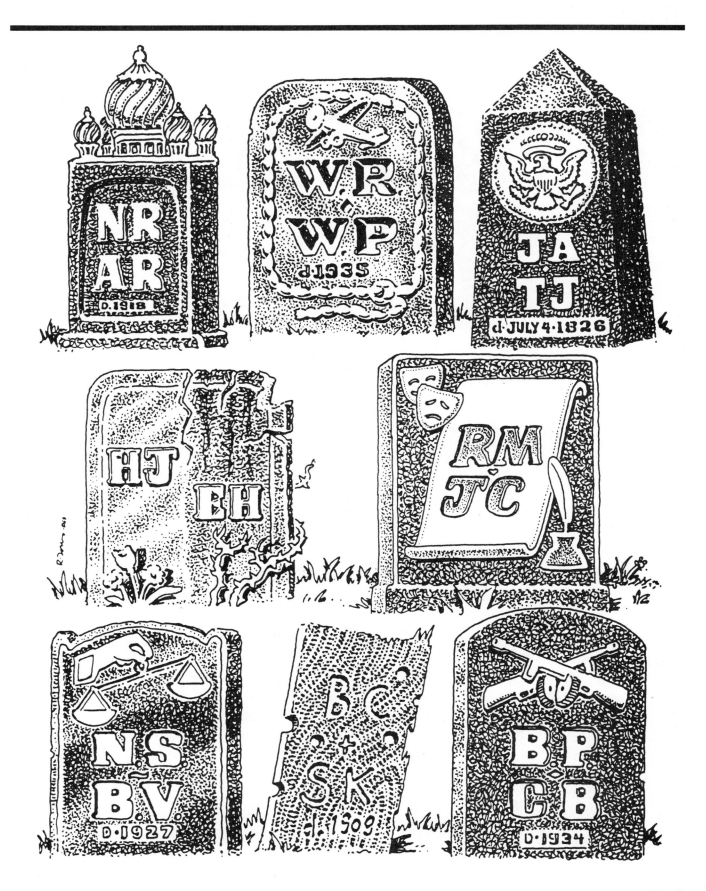

20. Sound track

Each of the sounds at the right is part of a name.
See if you can match them up with the other parts listed below.

___ Gibson

___ Aldrin

___ Torn

___ Iggy

___ Saul

___ Mancini

___ Alger

___ Craddock

___ Rubble

___ Goldberg

___ Maxwell

___ Sims

___ Crosby

___ Francis

___ Lardner

___ Wilhelm

___ Brown

___ Connie

___ Marin

___ Tommy

21. Art decode

Each of the numbered pairs of symbols at the right stands for a word below. (They don't look like the words they represent—they're just arbitrary designs.) See if you can decode the art.

___ backfire

___ housework

___ backhand

___ flypaper

___ hangover

___ handout

___ firefly

___ paperback

___ hangout

___ overhand

___ paperwork

___ firework

___ housefly

___ overhang

___ outhouse

ARE YOU A GOOD WITNESS?

Do you *observe* or do you just merely *look?* When your eye takes in a scene, does it register detail or does it just gather a fleeting, vague impression? The following test is designed to see how well you can report the facts.

Look at the picture below for just two minutes. Try to remember as much as you can! At the end of two minutes stop, and turn to the next page. You then get four minutes to answer the twenty questions about this picture.

You score 5 points for each correct answer. A score of 50 is passing; 60 is good; 70 is very good; 80 is excellent; 90 is brilliant. If you get 100, rent yourself out as a "private eye."

TIME LIMIT: FOUR MINUTES

1, On what floor was the fire?......~~........~~...........

2. On what street? .....~~........~~...........

3. What time of the day did the fire take place?......~~....~~.........

4. Were the firemen pumping water into the building?...........

5. Did the woman standing in the window have a baby in her arms?...........

6. What was the street number of the bakery store?...........

7. Was the policeman blowing his whistle?...........

8. Which tradesman used a bicycle for deliveries?...*Butcher*...........

9. How many firemen were on the job?...........

10. Were there more than fifteen people on the scene?...........

11. Was the jeweler's first name Charles?...........

12. Were there any windows facing South Street?...........

13. From what state was the automobile?...........

14. Was it a convertible?...........

15. How many fire engines were there?...........

16. Was there an exit on South Street?...........

17. Was the butcher bald?...........

18. Was there a dog anywhere on the scene?...........

19. Were there any vacant apartments in the burning buildings?...........

20. Was it wintertime?...........

$$1 \times 8 + 1 = 9$$
$$12 \times 8 + 2 = 98$$
$$123 \times 8 + 3 = 987$$
$$1234 \times 8 + 4 = 9876$$
$$12345 \times 8 + 5 = 98765$$
$$123456 \times 8 + 6 = 987654$$
$$1234567 \times 8 + 7 = 9876543$$
$$12345678 \times 8 + 8 = 98765432$$
$$123456789 \times 8 + 9 = 987654321$$

22. Modifiers

Each of the words at the right has been modified to suggest a familiar two-word phrase or expression. The first phrase, for example, is "split ends." Can you figure out the rest?

1) _____

2) _____

3) _____

4) _____

5) _____

6) _____

7) _____

8) _____

9) _____

10) _____

11) _____

12) _____

1

2 APPEND/IX

3 chance

4 VALUE

5 S E B S L S G N I

6 Invalties royalties

7 RET'NA

8 CARTILAGE

9 ARTICLES

10 VARLU

11 songbards

12 EGO

23. Souper bowl

The names of 20 different ingredients appear in this bowl of alphabet soup. The letters of each ingredient are strung together in correct order. You'll find the word "cabbage," for example, along the top of the bowl, next to the spoon. See if you can find the rest. You must use all of the letters, but each of them only once.

1) _____

2) _____

3) _____

4) _____

5) _____

6) _____

7) _____

8) _____

9) _____

10) _____

11) _____

12) _____

13) _____

14) _____

15) _____

16) _____

17) _____

18) _____

19) _____

20) _____

24. Lip reading

Each of these mustaches grew out of one of the characters listed below. We've identified a few of them to start things off. See if you can match up the rest.

_____ Mark Twain

_____ Albert Einstein

__9__ Josef Stalin

_____ Salvador Dalí

_____ Charlie Chaplin

_____ Augustus Mutt

_____ Thomas E. Dewey

__10__ Lech Wałęsa

_____ Sonny Crockett

__7__ Martin Luther King

__1__ Stacy Keach

_____ Kaiser Wilhelm

_____ Edgar Allan Poe

_____ Adolf Hitler

_____ Groucho Marx

_____ J. Wellington Wimpy

_____ Rollie Fingers

__4__ Friedrich Nietzsche

25. Paint by numbers

Each of the numbers at right represents a color from the palette below. See if you can match them up.

___ white
___ red
_9_ dark blue
___ green
___ yellow
_8_ brown
___ black
___ golden brown
___ blue

26. Lots of luck

What is the fewest number of moves necessary to get the black car out of the lot? The vehicles may move forward or backward in a straight line only. (No packing, cramming or mere inching up.) And you must count *every* move, even if you shift the same vehicle more than once.

List the numbers of the vehicles, in order, in the space provided.

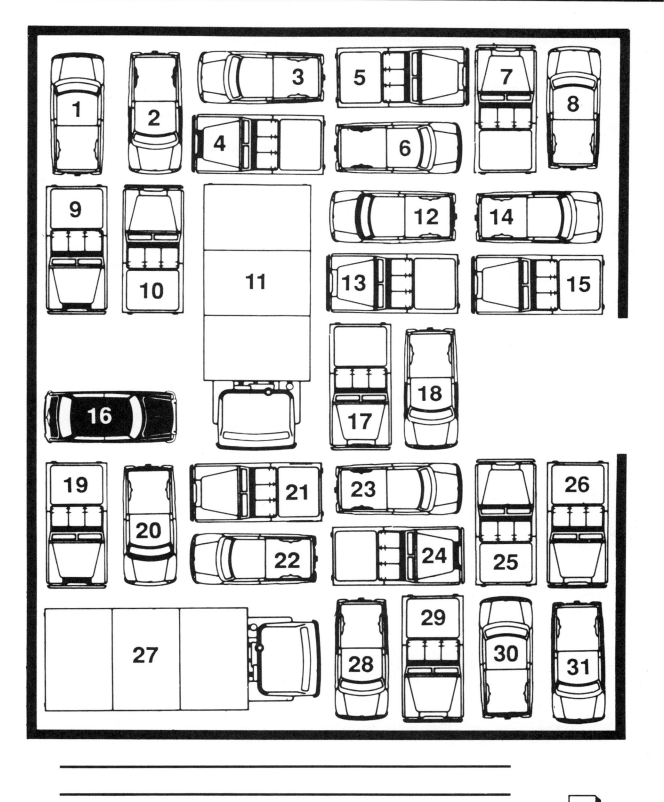

27. Borderline

What if places were shaped like their names? Well, you can see a few of the Florida Keys in the southeast corner of this map. See if you can name the rest.

They are all in appropriate geographic locations, more or less.

_____

_____

_____

_____

_____

_____

_____

_____

_____

_____

_____

_____

_____

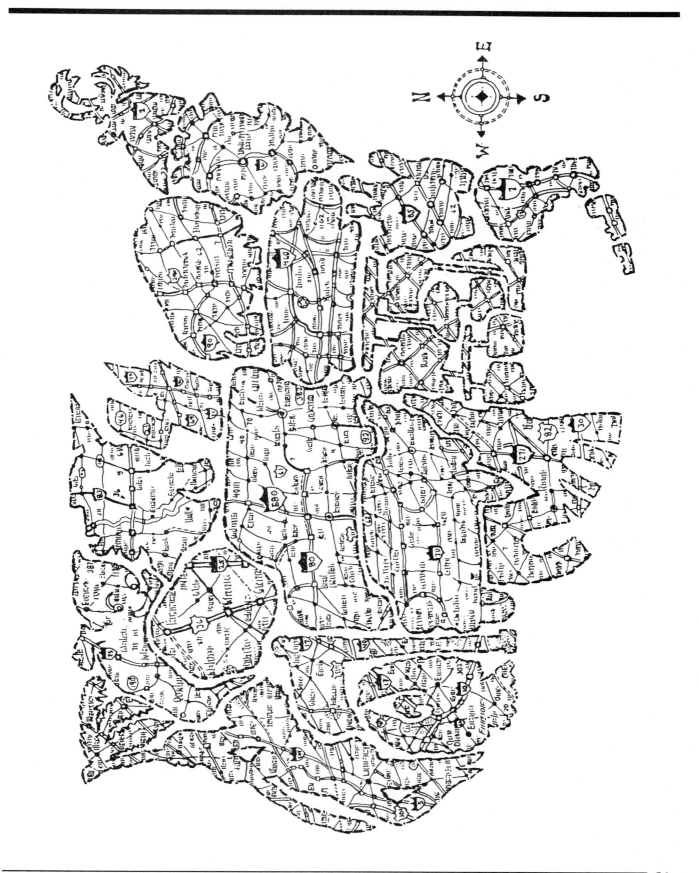

28. Going up?

Each of these elevators travels at the same speed and stops at every floor. Right now they're all going up, except the ones at the top, which are coming down. The cars reverse directions only at the top and bottom.

The object is to make your way from the ground floor via elevator number 1 to the ground floor via elevator number 7 by moving from car to car. You may switch from one elevator only to an adjacent elevator on the same floor. (For example, if you take car number 1 four floors, car number 2 will have traveled up two floors, then down two, and you can get aboard.) You may not, however, wait around on a floor for an elevator to arrive.

How many floors, total, must you travel to reach your goal? (Purists will try to solve this puzzle in their heads.)

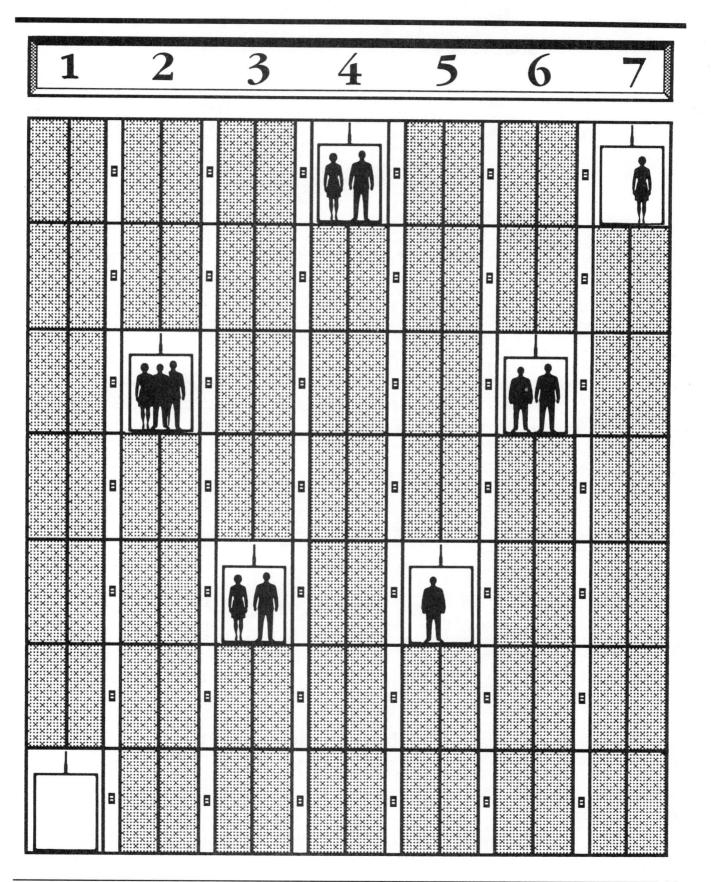

29. Negative space

Fourteen words — a total of 63 capital letters — are hidden in the maze at the right. Don't see them? Try coloring in the various shapes. Then list the words below.

1) _____
2) _____
3) _____
4) _____
5) _____
6) _____
7) _____
8) _____
9) _____
10) _____
11) _____
12) _____
13) _____
14) _____

30. First class

Each of the stamps at the right commemorates a US city whose ZIP code appears below. To pass your first class in postgraduate philately, all you have to do is match them up.

___ 89109

___ 19106

___ 38116

___ 90028

___ 08401

___ 94109

___ 20500

___ 10166

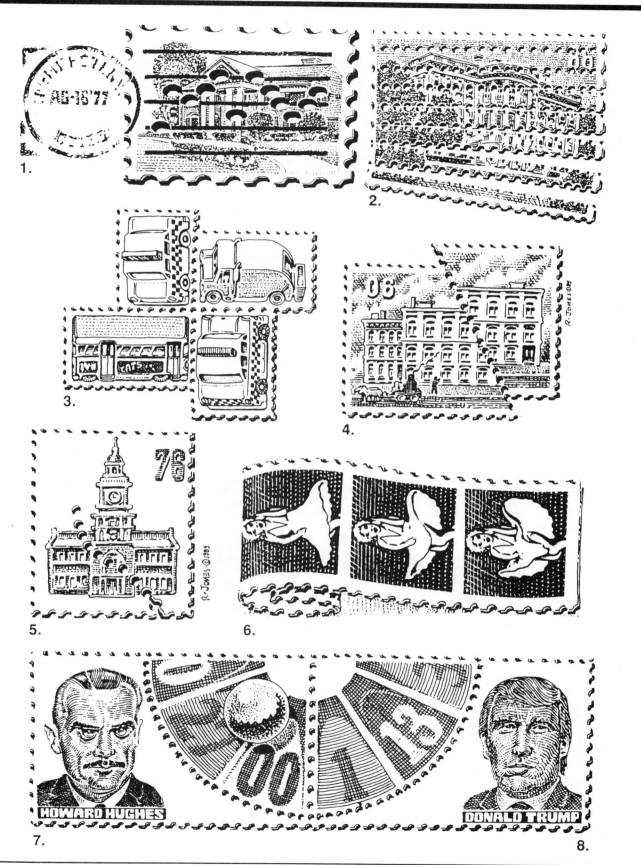

1.

2.

3.

4.

5.

6.

HOWARD HUGHES

DONALD TRUMP

7.

8.

31. Dress code

How many styles can you identify?

___ chemise

___ kilt

___ gaucho

___ blouson

___ flared

___ Empire

___ sheath

___ box pleats

___ knife pleats

___ dirndl

___ jumpsuit

___ wrap

___ princess

___ smock

___ short shorts

___ inverted pleat

___ gored

___ Bermuda shorts

___ walking shorts

___ knickers

___ bell bottoms

___ shift

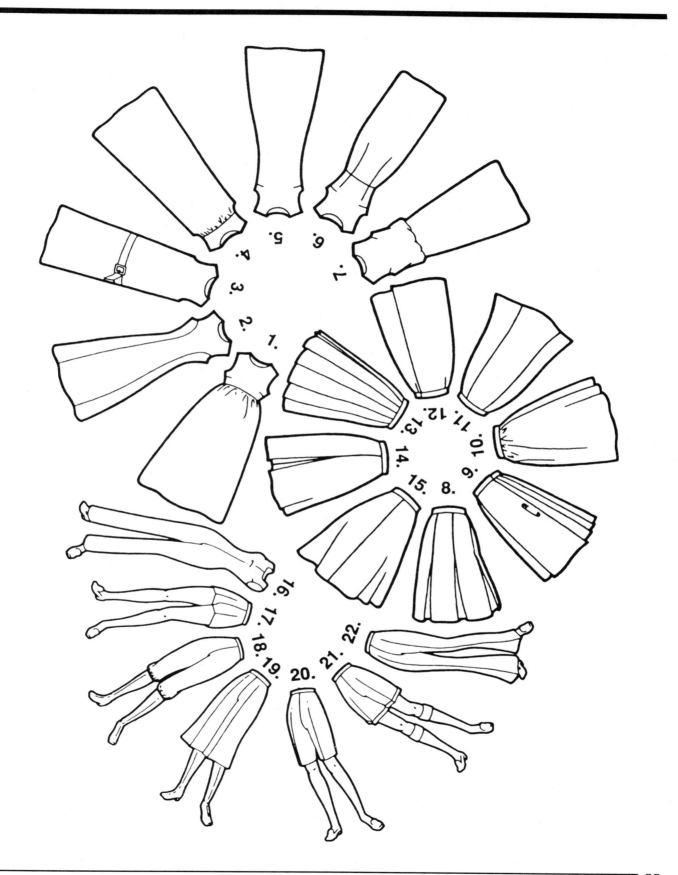

32. Understatements

Each of the titles in the left-hand column is an understatement of some artistic work associated with a person on the right. *Interplanetary Tiffs*, for example, is an understatement of *Star Wars*, by Lucas. See if you can match the rest.

Our thanks to Sidney E. Lind, professor emeritus at Brooklyn College, whose inspiration for this puzzle was *Real Genius* — well, a pretty good idea.

MAÑANA
URGENT!

1) The Chat _____ Sartre
2) 9 _____ Lewis
3) The Coincidence Maker _____ Spielberg
4) Back Road _____ Allman
5) Tropic of Herpes _____ Godard
6) Call Directory Assistance _____ Lucas
7) The Nine Suggestions _____ Miller
8) Gums _____ Chandler
9) Interplanetary Tiffs _____ Verne
10) NutraSweet, NutraSweet _____ Truffaut
11) Three Feet Up _____ O'Toole
12) Nibble a Grape _____ Ferber
13) The Light Nap _____ Michelangelo
14) Fellow Travelers _____ Edwards
15) Winded _____ Karloff
16) About Gerbils and Guys _____ Updike
17) 8 _____ Archies
18) Brunch at Sears _____ Joyce
19) Queasiness _____ Leonardo
20) Ugly Guy's Girlfriend _____ Capote
21) H.A.N.D. _____ Duke
22) Wound the Guitarist _____ Steinbeck
23) Modest Aspirations _____ Beatty
24) Dave _____ Byrds
25) The Penultimate Tea _____ Coppola
26) Midget _____ DeMille
27) Bunny Jog _____ Stallone
28) Murphys Sickbed _____ Fellini
29) Several Feet Under Water _____ Hitchcock
30) Larry of Kuwait _____ Dickens

33. House work

This is a *soko*, or Japanese warehouse; the name also refers to a popular puzzle from Osaka.

You are the *sokoban* (warehouseman) who's just been hired to remove the eight numbered crates that are scattered about inside. The crates are very heavy, and they don't have handles. You're strong enough to push them one at a time—you can't pull them—but you'll need a crate-sized space behind each box to work in. You may not rotate the crates, or climb over them, or squeeze between them. And no diagonal moves are allowed. If you push a crate into a corner or can't get behind it, it's stuck. Don't worry about the boxes once they've left the warehouse. A truck will cart each away to make room for the next.

What is the least amount of work required to accomplish your task? And how did you do it? To list the moves, write the number of the crate, followed by the direction (U for up, D for down, L for left, R for right), and then the number of squares moved (e.g., 7R1). Then add up the squares. Only full-square moves are allowed. You needn't record your own moves, just the crates'.

Moves

_____

_____

_____

_____

_____

_____

_____

Total squares: _____

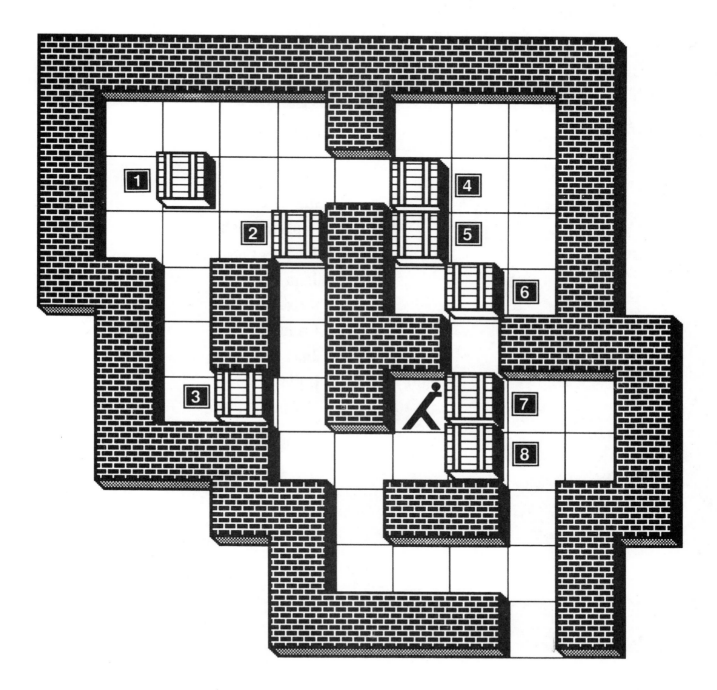

34. Foot work

You can figure out who walked on this fresh cement by examining the footprints, which are characteristic. But who stepped on it first, and in what order did the rest of them follow? We'd like you to number the list below chronologically.

— **Ironside**

— **Lassie**

— **Big Bird**

— **Captain Ahab**

— **Jacques Cousteau**

— **John Doe**

— **Kareem**

— **Friday**

— **Jane Doe**

— **Bigfoot**

— **Neil Armstrong**

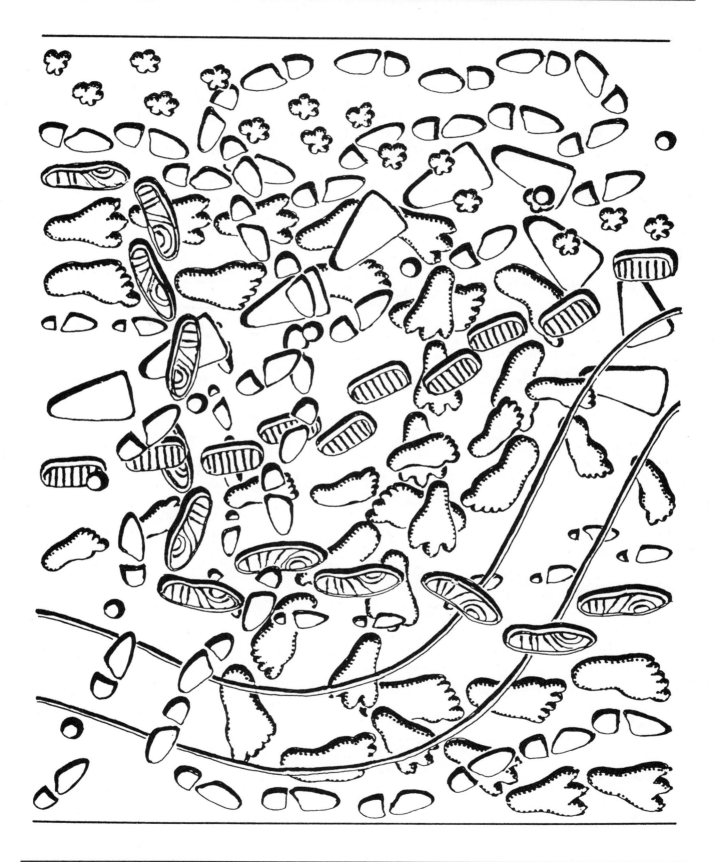

35. I-chart

How do optometrists test people who can't read?

Each of the images at the right is associated, by spelling or sound, with a letter of the alphabet. See how many you can identify. Then write the correct letters in the spaces below.

‾‾‾‾

‾‾‾‾‾‾

‾‾‾‾‾‾‾

‾‾‾‾‾‾‾‾

‾‾‾‾‾‾‾‾‾

‾‾‾‾‾‾‾‾‾‾

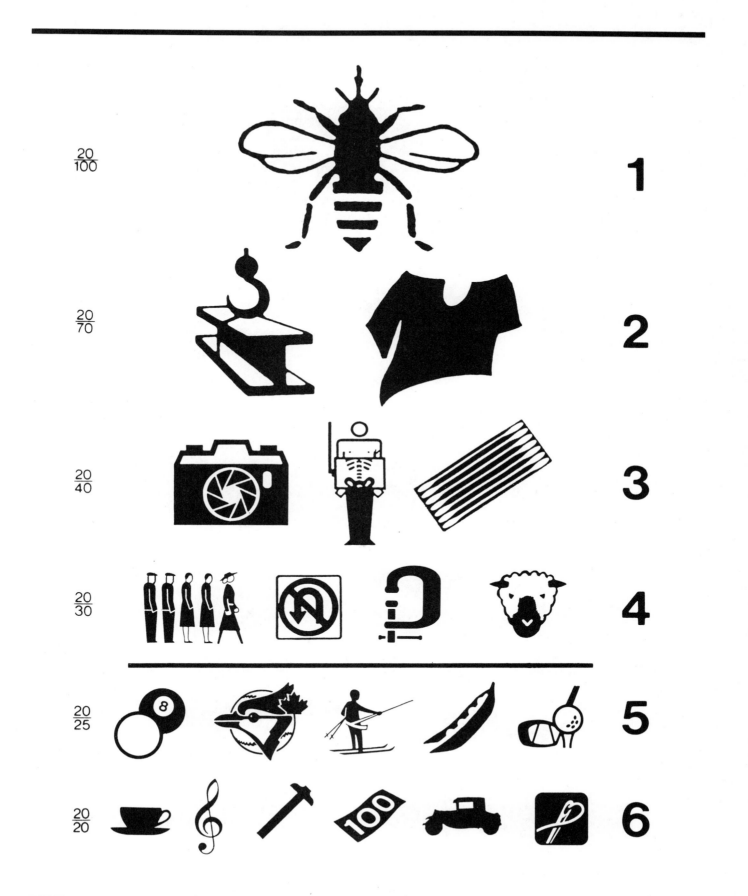

20/100 1

20/70 2

20/40 3

20/30 4

20/25 5

20/20 6

36. Gridlock

Starting in the blank square at the bottom of the grid and moving horizontally or vertically (but not diagonally), you'll need only 23 moves to reach a legal parking space. Show us the route.

You must follow the arrows wherever you encounter them. And no U-turns are allowed.

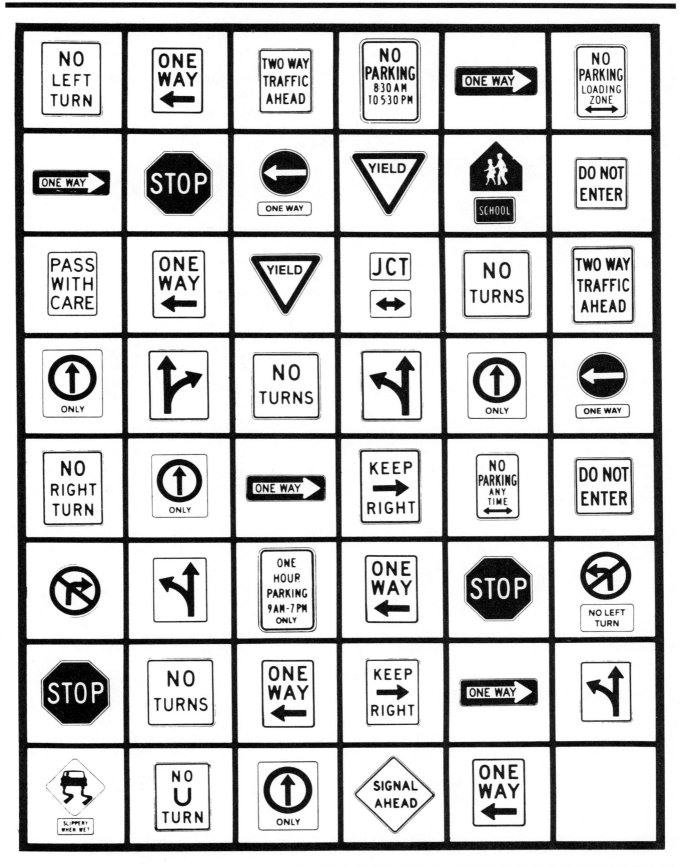

37. Sema-four?

Each of these pennants stands for a one-digit number.

We'd like you to translate the equations into conventional math and write them out below.

_____

_____

_____

_____

_____

_____

_____

_____

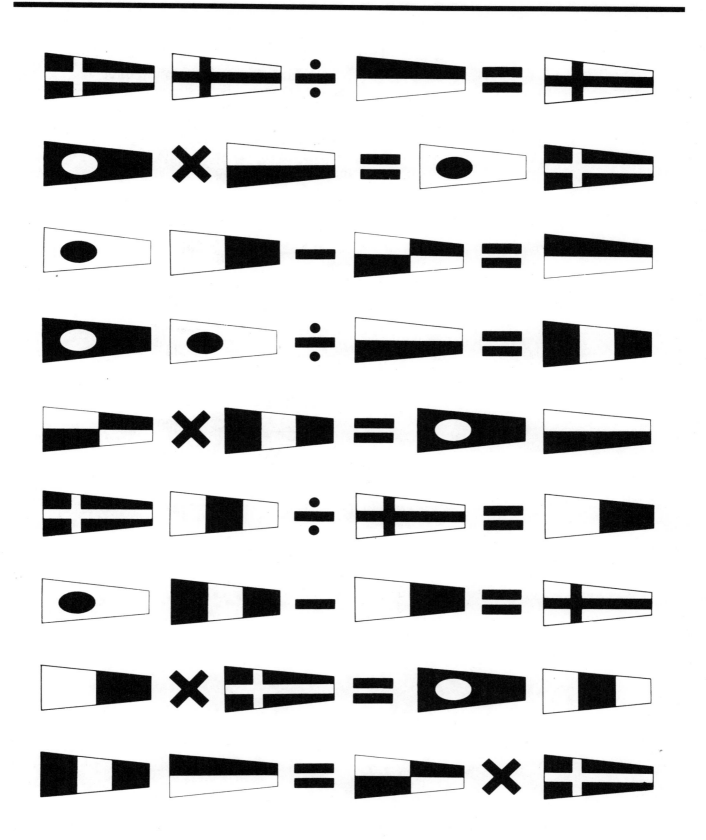

38. Roman times

There are several ways to interpret each of these problems, depending on whether the X's are Roman numerals or multiplication signs. (See example.) One of the solutions to each of the problems is given below. See if you can match everything up.

_____	**31,460**
_____	**900**
_____	**8,910**
_____	**126,000**
_____	**212,100**
_____	**6,000**
_____	**56,100**
_____	**231**
_____	**24,200**
_____	**381,500**

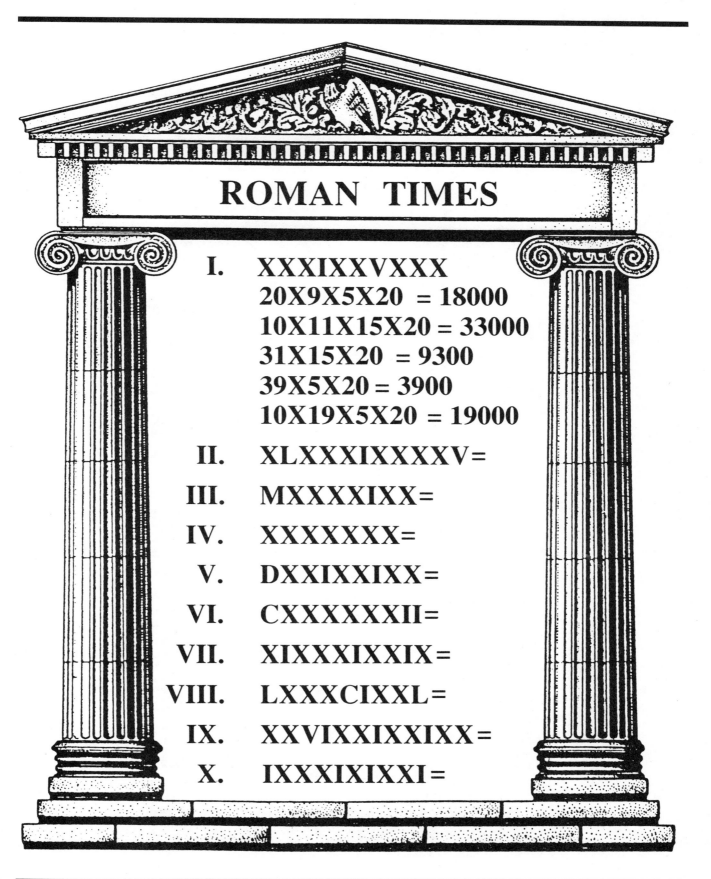

ROMAN TIMES

I. XXXIXXVXXX

20X9X5X20 = 18000
10X11X15X20 = 33000
31X15X20 = 9300
39X5X20 = 3900
10X19X5X20 = 19000

II. XLXXXIXXXXV=

III. MXXXXIXX=

IV. XXXXXXX=

V. DXXIXXIXX=

VI. CXXXXXXII=

VII. XIXXXIXXIX=

VIII. LXXXCIXXL=

IX. XXVIXXIXXIXX=

X. IXXXIXIXXI=

39. Blind date

We pasted a familiar poster on a set of Venetian blinds and then pulled the cord to reverse it. Can you identify the character in the picture?

_____

40. Mr. Baseball

Only wrestlers and organized-crime figures have better nicknames than baseball players. Bob Ferguson, a second baseman during baseball's early days, was nicknamed Death to Flying Things, presumably for his skill with a glove. Of course, he wasn't especially fond of birds, either.

Each of the ballplayers listed below has a sobriquet that's illustrated at the right. See if you can tag them correctly.

___ Dennis Boyd   ___ Jim Hunter

___ Ron Cey   ___ Mark Fidrych

___ Bob Uecker   ___ Stan Musial

___ Leroy Paige   ___ Joe Medwick

___ Bill Lee   ___ Dwight Gooden

___ Ty Cobb   ___ Harmon Killebrew

___ Sal Maglie   ___ Rich Gossage

___ Bill Skowron   ___ Greg Luzinski

___ Harry Simpson   ___ George Herman Ruth

___ Harold Traynor   ___ Ken Harrelson

___ Rogers Hornsby   ___ Reggie Jackson

___ Harry Walker   ___ Roger Clemens

1.

2.

3.

4.

5.

6.

7.

8.

9.

10.

11.

12.

13.

14.

15.

16.

17.

18.

19.

20.

21.

22.

23.

24.

41. Mugs

Each of these mugs represents a famous personality whose name begins or ends with "stein." List their names below.

1) _____

2) _____

3) _____

4) _____

5) _____

6) _____

7) _____

8) _____

9) _____

Each of the figures at the right is a word formed from the alphabet at the bottom. The letters are strung together in correct order.

See if you can figure the words out. Fill in your answers below.

1) _____
2) _____
3) _____
4) _____
5) _____
6) _____
7) _____
8) _____
9) _____
10) _____
11) _____
12) _____
13) _____
14) _____
15) _____
16) _____
17) _____
18) _____
19) _____
20) _____
21) _____
22) _____
23) _____
24) _____

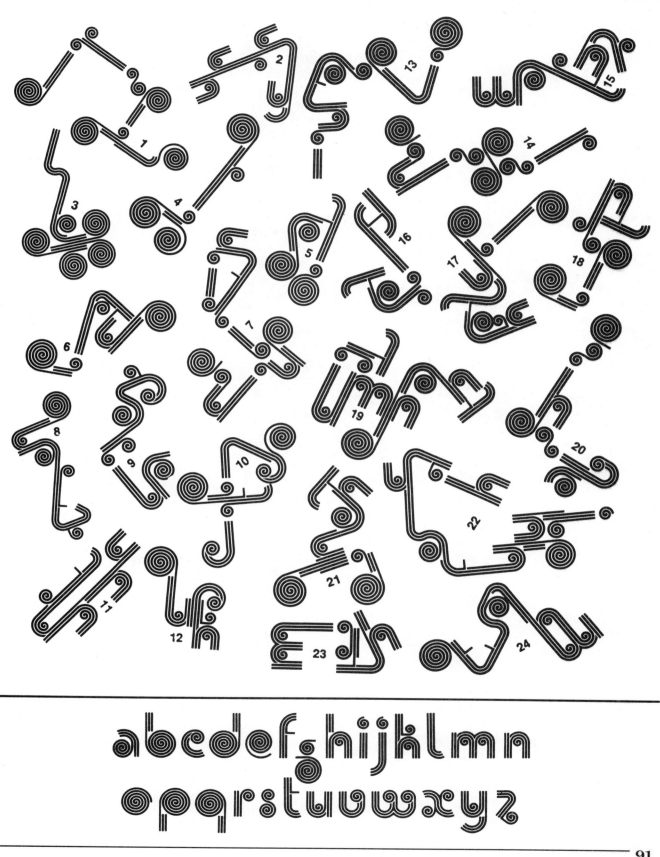

abcdefghijklmn
opqrstuvwxyz

43. Board work

Four chess pieces (two of them Kings) are hidden in the troughs of this warped chess board. There is only one square that each of these hidden pieces can occupy. Black's last move (N-KN6ch) tells you where one of them is. And with a little thought, you can deduce the locations of the rest. (For example, the White King could not be at QR3 because it would be under check from the Black Queen.)

Now it's White to move and mate in two.

White	**Black**
. . . .	**N-KN6ch**
_____	_____
_____	

44. Old Test.

This cryptogram was created by touch-typing a message on a Hebrew typewriter. (That is, we didn't look at the keys.) Can you decipher it?

No knowledge of Hebrew is required. Well, there *is* one thing you should know about the language.

_____

_____

_____

_____

_____

_____

אי קרקכסרק וד איק

משצק סכ וא בשרדקג

נשנקך

נקבשרדק איק רסרג

גוג איקרק בסמכסומג

איק רשמערשעק

סכ שרך איק קשראי

שמג כרסצ איקמבק

גוג איק רסרג

דכשאאקר איקצ שנרסשג

רפסמ איק כשבק

סכ שרך איק קשראי

45. Locations

Each of the logos at the right was designed to promote filmmaking in a city, state, or country listed below. (In fact, some are represented more than once.)

See if you can match them up, as shown.

__15__	**Australia (4)**
_____	**Israel**
_____	**Tokyo**
_____	**Italy**
_____	**Arabian Gulf States**
_____	**Banff**
_____	**Czechoslovakia**
_____	**England**
_____	**United States (2)**
_____	**Canada (2)**

1

2

3

4

5

6

7

8

9

10

11

12

13

14

15

46. C-2?

Each of these planes is one of a pair of identical aircraft, as seen from different vantage points.

See two? List each of the pairs of matching planes below.

a ——

b ——

c ——

d ——

e ——

f ——

g ——

h ——

i ——

j ——

k ——

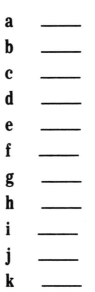

47. I-cues

We've dotted the two i's in "Miami" with a beach ball and a sun, which sort of characterize the location. Using the other i-cues provided, see if you can identify the rest of these appropriately dotted words.

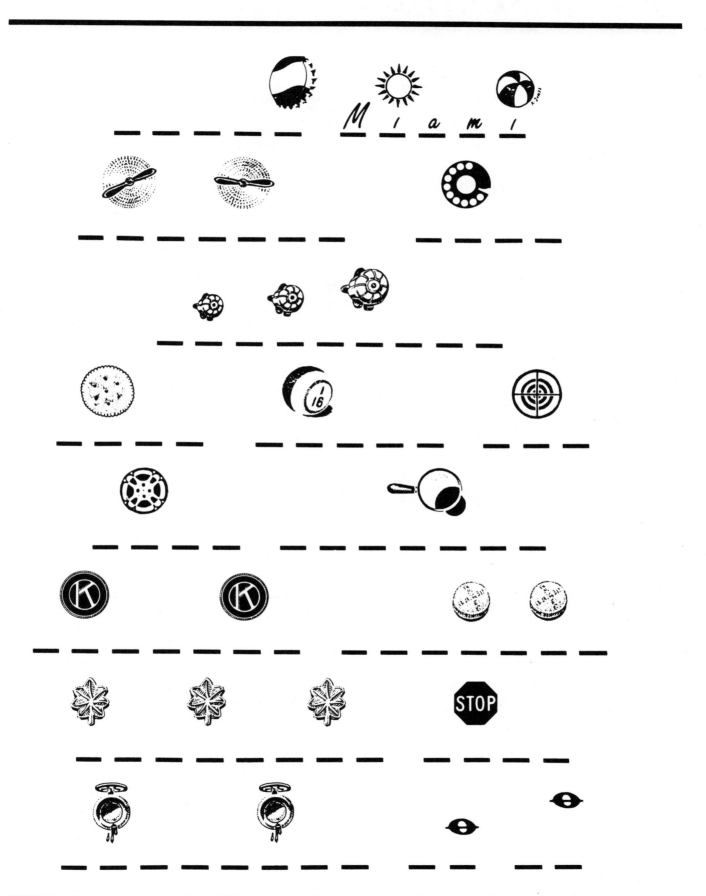

M i a m i

48. Medicine chest

"Honey, have you seen the Right Guard?"

Each of these containers holds a familiar product from your bathroom shelf. See how many you can identify.

1) _____
2) _____
3) _____
4) _____
5) _____
6) _____
7) _____
8) _____
9) _____
10) _____
11) _____
12) _____
13) _____
14) _____
15) _____
16) _____
17) _____
18) _____
19) _____
20) _____ *Selsun Blue* _____
21) _____
22) _____

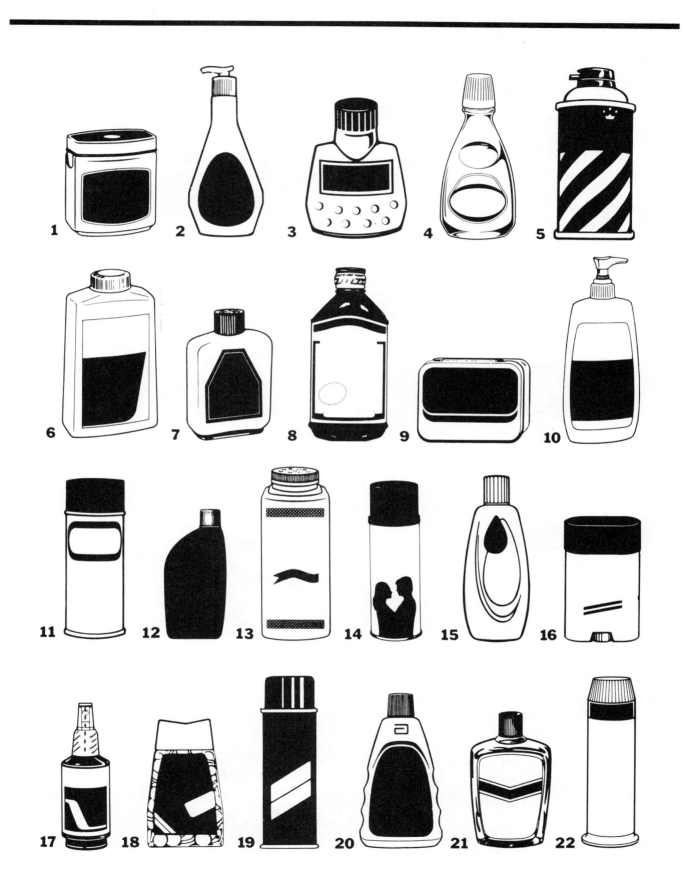

1

2

3

4

5

6

7

8

9

10

11

12

13

14

15

16

17

18

19

20

21

22

49. Classic hits

Drop a pfennig in the jukebox and try to match each of the lettered classical or operatic works with a numbered composer. You can enter your solutions on the buttons at the bottom.

Romantic Symphony	a 1	n 14	*New World Symphony*
Wagner			Saint-Saëns
The Seasons	b 2	o 15	*Resurrection Symphony*
Rimsky-Korsakov			J. Strauss
Thus Spake Zarathustra	c 3	p 16	*La Traviata*
Schubert			Holst
Scenes from Childhood	d 4	q 17	*Coffee Cantata*
Dvořák			Mozart
Die Fledermaus	e 5	r 18	*Peer Gynt*
Vivaldi			R. Strauss
Oedipus Rex	f 6	s 19	*Finlandia*
Chopin			Haydn
Symphonie fantastique	g 7	t 20	*Tales of Hoffmann*
Bach			Schumann
Organ Symphony	h 8	u 21	*Funeral March Sonata*
Puccini			Verdi
Ring of the Nibelungs	i 9	v 22	*Unfinished Symphony*
Mussorgsky			Handel
Choral Symphony	j 10	w 23	*The Four Seasons*
Stravinsky			Berlioz
Royal Fireworks Music	k 11	x 24	*La Bohème*
Mahler			Grieg
The Planets	l 12	y 25	*Scheherazade*
Bruckner			Beethoven
Don Giovanni	m 13	z 26	*Boris Godunov*
Sibelius			Offenbach

a b c d e f g h i j k l m
n o p q r s t u v w x y z

6

50. Silverwhere

Match each of the underlined utensils at the right with a numbered description appearing below.

1) Teaspoon
2) Table fork
3) Table knife
4) Tablespoon
5) Soup spoon
6) Salad fork
7) Lemon stick
8) Demitasse spoon
9) Long drink spoon
10) Nut spoon
11) Cheese knife
12) Cold meat fork
13) Pastry server
14) Melon spoon
15) Salad-serving fork
16) Sugar tongs
17) Carving fork
18) Carving knife
19) Table serving spoon
20) Table serving fork
21) Butter knife
22) Ice cream spoon
23) Soup ladle
24) Salt spoon
25) Salad-serving spoon
26) Punch ladle
27) Lobster fork
28) Snail tongs
29) Ice tongs
30) Spaghetti server

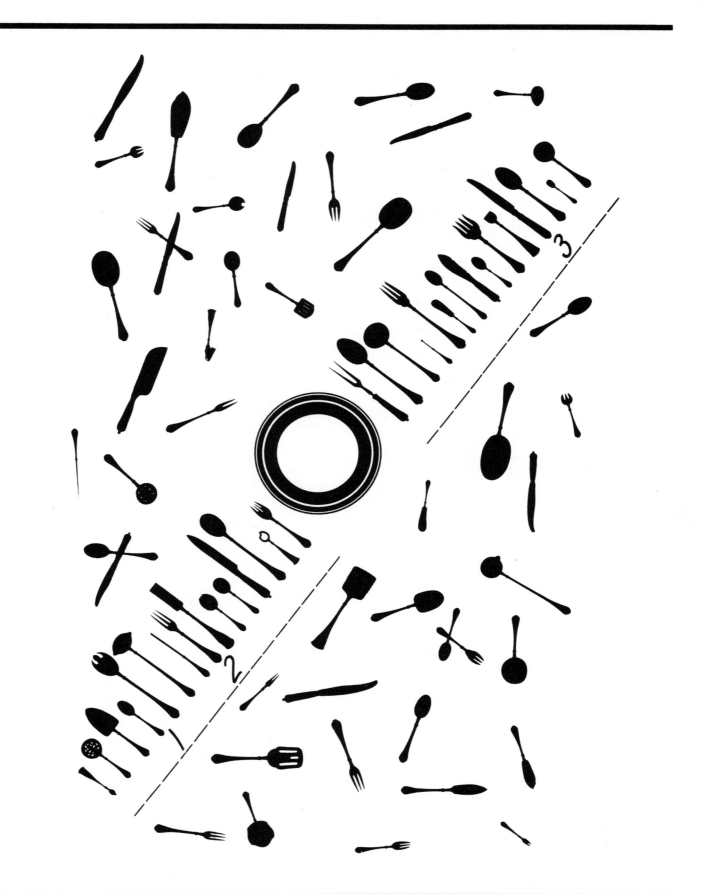

Solutions

1. Shake-up

1) Sandy — Chris
2) Chris — Jackie
3) Jackie — Pat
4) Sandy — Tracy
5) Dale — Chris
6) Sandy — Dale

2. Four-letter words

1) HULA
2) LAME
3) MEAL
4) ALTO
5) TOAD
6) ADZE
7) ZERO
8) ROPE
9) PESO
10) SOLO
11) LOCO
12) COLA
13) LAMA
14) MARE
15) RENO
16) NOTE
17) TEST
18) STEM
19) EMIR
20) IRIS

3. Mental blocks

The following patterns yield cubes
when properly folded:

A, D, E, G and H

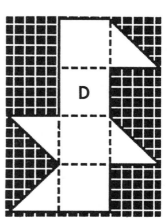

4. War games

13) British Invasion (Beatles)
18) Custody Battle (broken family)
14) Big Mac Attack (burger)
6) War on Poverty (patches)
9) Heart Attack (electrocardio-
gram)
17) Cold War (icicles)
8) Price Wars (markdown)
5) Star Wars (Darth Vader)
3) Armageddon (fragments)
4) Battle of the Sexes (gender
symbols)
12) Media Blitz (television sets)
11) Saturday Night Massacre (Nixon)
2) Political Campaign (donkey and
elephant)
1) War of the Worlds (radio broad-
cast)
16) Battle of Wits (thinkers)
10) Industrial Revolution (gears)
7) Invasion of the Body Snatchers
(pod)
15) Sexual Revolution ('60s slogan)

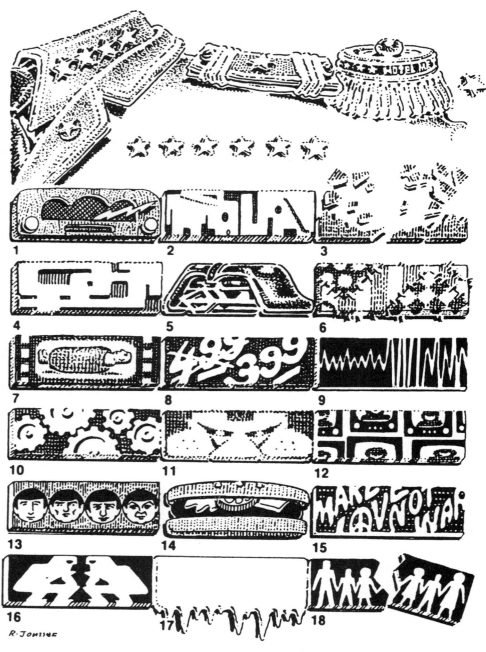

R·JONSSE

5. Fare game

1) 6
2) 9
3) 10
4) 1
5) 11
6) 8
7) 12
8) 4
9) 7
10) 2
11) 3
12) 5

MAPLE SYRUP should appear in the rustic typeface (CHOW MEIN), SALISBURY STEAK in the TV (dinner) face (VINDALOO), POPCORN in the marquee face (TANG), MOUSSAKA in the Greek face (MAPLE SYRUP), CHILI CON CARNE in the southwestern face (BORSCHT), CHOW MEIN in the Chinese face (KNISHES), SAUERKRAUT in the German face (BABA GANOOSH), KNISHES in the Hebrew face (MOUSSAKA), VINDALOO in the Indian face (SAUERKRAUT), TANG in the high-tech face (SALISBURY STEAK), BORSCHT in the Cyrillic face (POPCORN), and BABA GANOOSH in the Middle Eastern face (CHILI CON CARNE). Got it?

6. Odd ball

1) EYEBALL
2) MIRRORED BALL
3) GOLF BALL
4) ORANGE
5) WHIFFLE BALL
6) TENNIS BALL
7) BALL OF YARN
8) BILLIARD BALL
9) BLUEBERRY
10) THE EARTH
11) BASKETBALL
12) CHRISTMAS ORNAMENT
13) SOCCER BALL
14) EPCOT CENTER
15) BASEBALL
16) THE MOON

7. Lost and found

HOWLAND ISLAND (US)

0°48′N 176°38′W

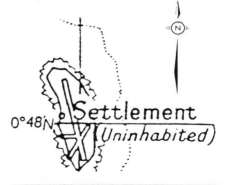

8. Paint can

9. Package deal

The parking meter was a red herring. The boxes and bags provided almost all the clues necessary to solve the puzzle.

The woman started by removing a large spotted box from the trunk of her car (1) and carried it into the coat store through the revolving front door (2). She returned whatever was in the box and left the store with a spotted bag (3), crossed the street, and entered the watch-repair shop (4). She left the watch-repair shop with a checkered box and the spotted bag (5), and visited the clothes shop, leaving with a third, striped bag (6). Then she visited the tailor (7), left the spotted bag, and walked back across the street to the toy store (8), where she bought a stuffed Garfield, which she placed in the trunk of the car (9).

The panels in the puzzle were:

6	3	5
9	7	2
4	1	8

10. With E's

20 American Typewriter	13 Pin Ball
11 Neon	25 Sampler
2 Ivy League	3 Rope
5 Old English	19 Fleurdon
27 Stack	14 Smile
9 Brush Script	26 Data
24 Domino	22 Xerxes
16 L.C.D.	15 Rickshaw
29 Scimitar	17 Marquee
12 Croissant	30 Lariat
8 Stencil	21 Quicksilver
23 Television	1 Shatter
6 Masquerade	10 Rustic
4 Rush	7 Chromium One
28 Ringlet	18 Fingers

11. Marquee de Sade

1) Melvin and Howard the Duck Soup
2) Sleeping Beauty and The Beast from 20,000 Fathoms
3) King of Hearts of the West Side Story
   (King of Kong Island of Love Story)
   (King Solomon of Broadway to Hollywood Story)
4) Dirty Dancing in the Dark Passage
5) Dr. No Way Out of Africa
6) Watership Down and Out in Beverly Hills Cop
7) Starting Over the Top Gun
8) ... And Justice for All the King's [or President's] Men of Boys Town
   (... And Justice for All That Money Can Buy Me That Town)
   (... And Justice for All the Way, Boys Town)
   (And So They Were Married to the Mob Town)
   (And Baby Makes Three Wise Girls About Town)
9) A Patch of Blue Water, White Death Wish

10) The Big Easy Come, Easy Go West
    (The Big Red One Man's Way Out West)
    (The Big Night Passage West)
11) The Blackboard Jungle Jim Thorpe — All American
12) Bronco Billy the Kid Galahad
    (Bronco Billy: Portrait of a Street Kid Galahad)
13) Blume in Love Me Tender Mercies
14) Trading Places in The Heart Is a Lonely Hunter
15) April Love at First Bite the Bullet
16) Anne of the Thousand Days of Heaven Can Wait
17) Who Framed Roger Rabbit, Run Silent, Run Deep

18) ... And God Created Woman of The Year of Living Dangerously
19) Dinner at Eight Million Ways to Die Hard
20) Bright Lights, Big City of Women in Love
21) Talk Radio Days of Wine and Roses
    (Talk About a Stranger in My Bed of Roses)
22) Fool for Love and Death Race [or Ray] 2000
23) They Died with Their Boots On the Beach Blanket Bingo
24) Anatomy of a Murder by Death on the Nile
25) The Elephant Man Friday the 13th

12. See shells?

1) RAZOR CLAM
2) PERIWINKLE
3) QUAHOG
4) CONCH
5) SAND DOLLAR
6) OYSTER
7) BARNACLE
8) COWRY
9) ABALONE
10) SCALLOP

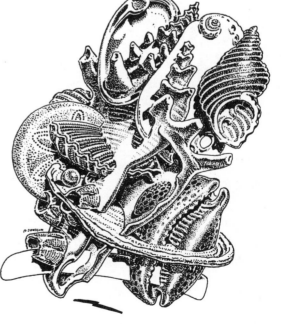

13. Jigsquare

When you cut out the jigsaw puzzle and put it together, you get another jigsaw. And when you put that together, you get Albert Einstein (not Mark Twain or Albert Schweitzer).

Here's the original puzzle, the intermediate solution, and the final result.

14. Blots

9   The Friendly Chickens
11   The Butterfly
3   Fishing for Shadow-Fish
6   A South Sea Idol
15   The Butterfly Man
4   The Grenadier
13   A Fanciful Elk
12   Miss F.M. De Lisle
14   A Glad Return
10   The Cathode (X-ray)
8   Queen Beetle
5   King Beetle
1   Good Breeding
16   The Washerwomen
2   The Mirror
7   Our Pet

15. Final round

What is
$283,200?

You'd have $17,800 at the end of Round One (assuming the Double Jeopardy question was in the $100 row, and you answered it last) and $141,600 at the end of Round Two (assuming both Double Jeopardy questions were in the $200 row and you answered them last). According to our sources at Merv Griffin Enterprises, a contestant may participate in Final Jeopardy even if both of his or her opponents have been eliminated.

You had to phrase your response as a question, remember?

THIS SUM
IS THE
LARGEST DOLLAR
AMOUNT
A CONTESTANT CAN WIN
IN A STANDARD GAME
OF
JEOPARDY!

16. Cereal killer

15 ALPHA-BITS
 3 CORN POPS
 7 CRISPIX
11 RICE KRISPIES
16 CORN FLAKES
 4 MUESLIX
10 HONEY SMACKS
 5 FROOT LOOPS
 6 GRAPE-NUTS
12 FROSTED MINI-WHEATS
 1 RAISIN BRAN
14 PRODUCT 19
13 NUT & HONEY CRUNCH
 8 FROSTED FLAKES
 2 ALL-BRAN
 9 SPECIAL K

17. Vase to vase

1) u - l	2) f - c	3) x - p
4) i - e	5) s - d	6) j - n
7) w - b	8) q - v	9) m - h
10) g - o	11) r - a	12) k - t

Fearless Fosdick ("the ideel of every red-blooded American boy") was Al Capp's parody of Chester Gould's cartoon detective Dick Tracy. The top-hatted character on every anniversary issue of The New Yorker is named Eustace Tilley.

18. Oversight

Aykroyd-Belushi
Masters-Johnson
Crusoe-Friday
Mason-Dixon
Desi-Lucy
Donny-Marie
Bogart-Bacall
Mutt-Jeff
Burns-Allen
Jonah-whale
Lewis-Clark
Lincoln-Douglas
Dukakis-Bentsen
Gumby-Pokey
George-Martha
Cain-Abel
Nixon-Agnew
Taylor-Burton
Bob-Ray

19. Dead letters

1) Czar Nicholas II and Czarina Alexandra Romanov
2) Will Rogers and Wiley Post
3) Presidents John Adams and Thomas Jefferson
4) Henry Jekyll and Edward Hyde
5) Romeo Montague and Juliet Capulet
6) Nicola Sacco and Bartolomeo Vanzetti
7) Butch Cassidy (George LeRoy) and the Sundance Kid (Harry Longabaugh)
8) Bonnie Parker and Clyde Barrow

20. Sound track

20	(Hoot) Gibson
17	(Buzz) Aldrin
6	(Rip) Torn
19	Iggy (Pop)
8	Saul (Bellow)
11	(Boom Boom) Mancini
12	Alger (Hiss)
18	(Crash) Craddock
13	(Bamm Bamm) Rubble
7	(Whoopi) Goldberg
3	(Slap) Maxwell
5	(Zoot) Sims
9	(Bing) Crosby
2	Francis (Crick)
1	(Ring) Lardner
14	Wilhelm (Klink)
4	(Rap) Brown
10	Connie (Chung)
15	(Cheech) Marin
16	Tommy (Chong)

Edward "Hoot" Gibson was a cowboy and silent-film star. But lots of people forget H. "Rap" Brown, the '60s radical, too. (It was he, Hubert Geroid Brown, who said, "Violence is as American as cherry pie." Remember?) And Francis Crick received a Nobel Prize for his work (with James Watson) on DNA.

21. Art decode

15 backfire
3 housework
8 backhand
7 flypaper
13 hangover
14 handout
5 firefly
10 paperback
6 hangout
1 overhand
11 paperwork
4 firework
12 housefly
9 overhang
2 outhouse

7.   8.

22. Modifiers

1) split ends
2) ruptured (or burst) appendix
3) fat chance
4) crushed velvet
5) mixed blessings
6) divided loyalties
7) detached retina
8) torn cartilage
9) broken promises
10) half-baked
11) dislocated (or separated) shoulder
12) inflated ego

23. Souper bowl

The ingredients in the bowl were (in no particular order):

1) ONIONS
2) LENTILS
3) CARROTS
4) PEAS
5) CABBAGE
6) SCALLIONS
7) OKRA
8) SPINACH
9) LEEKS
10) PARSNIPS
11) CORN
12) ESCAROLE
13) KOHLRABI
14) ASPARAGUS
15) CELERY
16) KALE
17) ZUCCHINI
18) GARBANZOS
19) TURNIPS
20) BROCCOLI

24. Lip reading

15   Mark Twain
 5   Albert Einstein
 9   Josef Stalin
11   Salvador Dali
 2   Charlie Chaplin
13   Augustus Mutt
 6   Thomas E. Dewey
10   Lech Walesa
17   Sonny Crockett
 7   Martin Luther King
 1   Stacy Keach
14   Kaiser Wilhelm
 8   Edgar Allan Poe
12   Adolf Hitler
16   Groucho Marx
18   J. Wellington Wimpy
 3   Rollie Fingers
 4   Friedrich Nietzsche

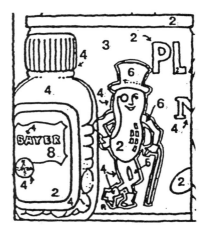

25. Paint by numbers

<u>4</u> white
<u>1</u> red
<u>9</u> dark blue
<u>5</u> green
<u>2</u> yellow
<u>8</u> brown
<u>6</u> black
<u>7</u> golden brown
<u>3</u> blue

26. Lots of luck

If it took you 45 moves to solve "Lots of Luck," you're smarter than many of our readers, which is very smart indeed. But not smart enough. You don't have to move autos 3 and 5 to extricate the black car.

The shortest solution is: 25, 26, 23, 24, 28, 29, 27, 19, 20, 21, 22, 11, 12, 13, 17, 18, 28, 29, 23, 24, 30, 31, 27, 11, 16, 9, 10, 1, 2, 4, 6, 17, 18, 28, 29, 16, 11, 27, 30, 31, 25, 26 and 16.

(Some people count the last move twice, but we don't hold that against them.)

Shortest solution: 43 moves.

27. Borderline

Caribou
    (Maine)
Frankfort
    (Kentucky)
Buffalo
    (New York)
Flint
    (Michigan)
Dodge City
    (Kansas)
Casper
    (Wyoming)
Flagstaff
    (Arizona)
Paris
    (Texas)

Elizabeth
    (New Jersey)
Bowling Green
    (Kentucky)
Mobile
    (Alabama)
Davenport
    (Iowa)
Bismarck
    (North Dakota)
Boulder
    (Colorado)
Phoenix
    (Arizona)
Tarzana
    (California)

The Florida Keys were used as examples.

We accept: Moosehead (a lake, really); Queens, Princess Anne (Maryland), and the District of Columbia; Brunswick (Maryland); Lincoln, El Dorado (Kansas), De Soto (Missouri), and Cadillac Ranch; Kaiser (Wisconsin); and Palm Springs.

We do not accept: Troy (Helen?), Los Angeles, Austin, Charlotte, Little Rock (much too far from Boulder), or Chevy Chase, among others.

28. Going up?

Take elevator number 1 up four floors, elevator 2 down four floors and up one, and elevator 3 down one floor and up four. At this point, elevators 3, 4, and 5 are all on the same floor (the fifth), and you have two options:

a) Take elevator 4 down four floors and up two, take elevator 5 down one, take elevator 6 up four floors, and take elevator 7 down five floors.

b) move from elevator 3 to elevator 4, and from 4 to 5 (all still on the fifth floor); then take elevator 5 up one floor, elevator 6 down four, and elevator 7 up five and down six.

Either way, the answer is 30.

The IBM Model 4381 prefers solution *a*, but somehow it seems less elegant. (Why travel six floors to reach an elevator that's already next to you?) Then again, the 11-floor move in route *b* isn't exactly a work of art.

29. Negative space

The 14 words are:

EEL   CELTIC
ELOPE   FELT
LICIT   LIFT
PLOT   POSIT
SECT   SITE
SPOIL   STILT
TIFF   TOPIC

30. First class

7) 89109 (Las Vegas)
5) 19106 (Philadelphia)
1) 38116 (Memphis)
6) 90028 (Hollywood)
8) 08401 (Atlantic City)
4) 94109 (San Francisco)
2) 20500 (Washington, DC)
3) 10166 (New York City)

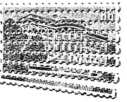

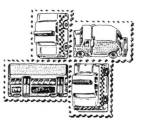

ZIP code numbers are higher the farther west one travels, which should have provided a few clues. The Memphis stamp features an engraving of Graceland, along with a postmark commemorating Elvis's death (August 8, 1977). The perforations on the cancellation are the opening notes from "Love Me Tender." The DC stamp is shredded. The New York City stamps are gridlocked. The (19)06-cent San Francisco stamp is perforated along an earthquake fault line. The Philadelphia stamp shows Independence Hall, with perforations like the crack in the Liberty Bell. The coil of Hollywood stamps features frames of film from *Some Like It Hot*. Howard Hughes and Donald Trump are pictured on the Vegas and Atlantic City stamps respectively.

31. Dress code

3 chemise
9 kilt
19 gaucho
7 blouson
15 flared
1 Empire
6 sheath
8 box pleats
13 knife pleats
10 dirndl
16 jumpsuit
12 wrap
2 princess
4 smock
17 short shorts
14 inverted pleat
11 gored
20 Bermuda shorts
21 walking shorts
18 knickers
22 bell bottoms
5 shift

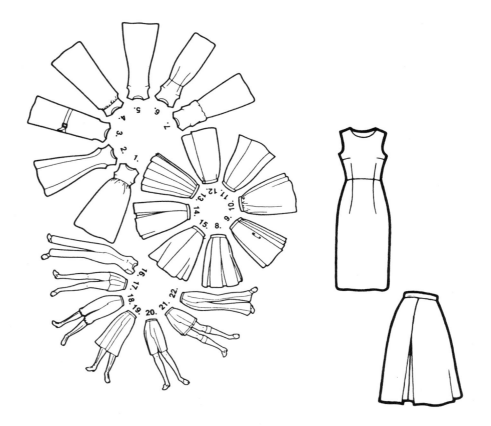

32. Understatements

19) Sartre *(Queasiness/Nausea)*
4) Lewis *(Back Road/Main Street)*
8) Spielberg *(Gums/Jaws)*
12) Allman *(Nibble a Grape/Eat a Peach)*
15) Godard *(Winded/Breathless)*
9) Lucas *(Interplanetary Tiffs/Star Wars)*
5) Miller *(Tropic of Herpes/Tropic of Cancer)*
13) Chandler *(The Light Nap/The Big Sleep)*
29) Verne *(Several Feet Under Water/20,000 Leagues Under the Sea*
22) Truffaut *(Wound the Guitarist/Shoot the Piano Player)*

30) O'Toole *(Larry of Kuwait/Lawrence of Arabia)*
26) Ferber *(Midget/Giant)*
24) Michelangelo *(Dave/David)*
2) Edwards *(9/10)*
20) Karloff *(Ugly Guy's Girlfriend/Bride of Frankenstein)*
27) Updike *(Bunny Jog/Rabbit Run)*
10) Archies *(NutraSweet, Nutrasweet/Sugar, Sugar)*
28) Joyce *(Murphys Sickbed/Finnegans Wake)*
25) Leonardo *(The Penultimate Tea/The Last Supper)*
18) Capote *(Brunch at Sears/Breakfast at Tiffany's)*
3) Duke *(The Coincidence Maker/The Miracle Worker)*

16) Steinbeck *(About Gerbils and Guys/Of Mice and Men)*
14) Beatty *(Fellow Travelers/Reds)*
11) Byrds *(Three Feet Up/Eight Miles High)*
1) Coppola *(The Chat/The Conversation)*
7) DeMille *(The Nine Suggestions/The Ten Commandments)*
21) Stallone *(H.A.N.D./F.I.S.T.)*
17) Fellini *(8/8½)*
6) Hitchcock *(Call Directory Assistance/Dial M for Murder)*
23) Dickens *(Modest Aspirations/Great Expectations)*

33. House work

Moves (41)
7R1, 6U1, 7L1, 8R1, 2U1, 2D1, 4R1, 4L1, 7D1, 8D4 (out), 7R1, 7D4 (out), 6D4, 6R1, 6D4 (out), 2U1, 2D1, 4R1, 4D5, 4R1, 4D4 (out), 2U1, 2R3, 2D5, 2R1, 2D4 (out), 5U1, 5R1, 5D5, 5R1, 5D4 (out), 1R5, 1D5, 1R1, 1D4 (out), 3R1, 3U4, 3R3, 3D5, 3R1, and 3D4 (out).
Total squares: 99

"House Work" is a puzzle of chesslike complexity. Many people start out by moving crate number 8 to the right one square and then down four (8R1, 8D4...). But moving 8 to the right eliminates the possibility of getting behind it (at least until you move crate 7).

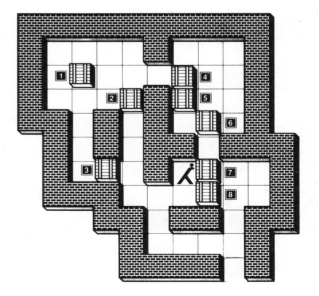

34. Foot work

6 Ironside
10 Lassie
2 Big Bird
11 Captain Ahab
4 Jacques Cousteau
9 John Doe
7 Kareem
5 Friday
3 Jane Doe
1 Bigfoot
8 Neil Armstrong

In order: 1) Bigfoot, 2) Big Bird, 3) Jane Doe, 4) Jacques Cousteau, 5) Friday, 6) Ironside, 7) Kareem, 8) Neil Armstrong, 9) John Doe, 10) Lassie and 11) Captain Ahab.

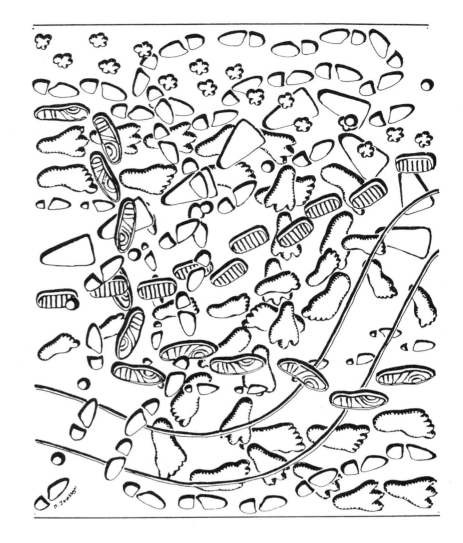

35. I-chart

1) bee
2) I-beam, T-shirt
3) f-stop, X-ray, Q-tip
4) queue, No U-turn, C-clamp, ewe
5) cue ball, Toronto Blue Jays, T-bar, pea pod, tee
6) teacup, G clef, T-square, C-note, Model T Ford, eye of needle)

("A" or "T" is okay for the Ford. It's hard to tell the difference in the silhouette.)

36. Gridlock

There are two ways to solve the puzzle, depending on the time of day. And both require 23 moves.

Between 9 a.m. and 5:30 p.m. you have to use the parking space in the third row from the bottom of the grid. And between 7 p.m. and 8:30 a.m. you have to use the parking space in the top row.

You have your choice of spaces (both are legal) between 5:30 p.m. and 7 p.m. On the other hand, it is absolutely impossible to solve the puzzle between 8:30 and 9 in the morning.

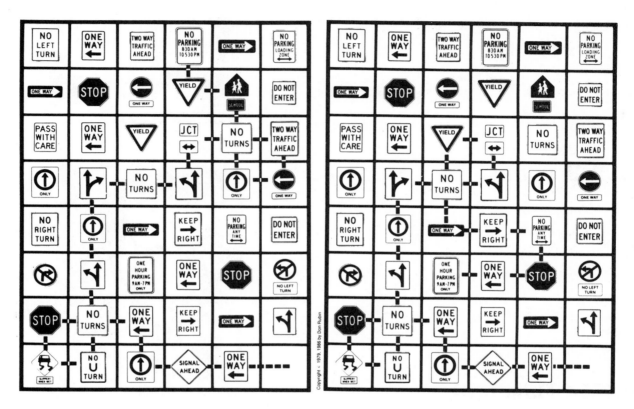

37. Sema-four?

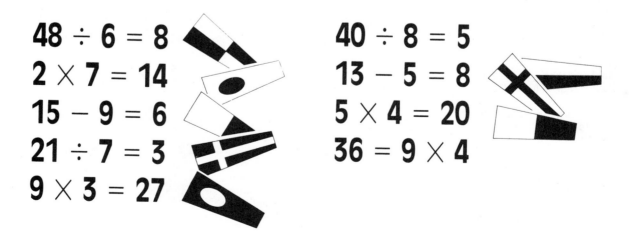

$$48 \div 6 = 8$$
$$2 \times 7 = 14$$
$$15 - 9 = 6$$
$$21 \div 7 = 3$$
$$9 \times 3 = 27$$

$$40 \div 8 = 5$$
$$13 - 5 = 8$$
$$5 \times 4 = 20$$
$$36 = 9 \times 4$$

38. Roman times

IX) 31,460 (26 x 11 x 11 x 10)
IV) 900 (30 x 30)
VII) 8,910 (11 x 10 x 9 x 9)
II) 126,000 (40 x 21 x 10 x 15)
III) 212,100 (1010 x 21 x 10)
I) 6,000 (20 x 1 x 15 x 20)
V) 56,100 (510 x 1 x 11 x 10)
X) 231 (1 x 21 x 1 x 11)
VI) 24,200 (110 x 10 x 22)
VIII) 381,500 (70 x 109 x 50)

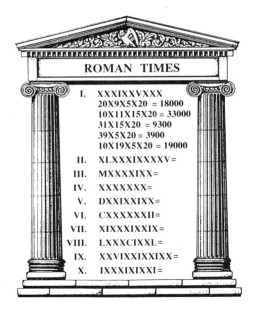

ROMAN TIMES

I. XXXIXXVXXX
   20X9X5X20 = 18000
   10X11X15X20 = 33000
   31X15X20 = 9300
   39X5X20 = 3900
   10X19X5X20 = 19000
II. XLXXXIXXXXV=
III. MXXXXIXX=
IV. XXXXXXX=
V. DXXIXXIXX=
VI. CXXXXXXII=
VII. XIXXXIXXIX=
VIII. LXXXCIXXL=
IX. XXVIXXIXXIXX=
X. IXXXIXIXXI=

39. Blind date

Jimmy Stewart

(as L.B. Jeffries in Hitchcock's *Rear Window*)

40. Mr. Baseball

18) Dennis "Oil Can" Boyd
1) Ron "The Penguin" Cey
21) Bob Uecker, "Mr. Baseball"
15) Leroy "Satchel" Paige
20) Bill "The Spaceman" Lee
6) Ty Cobb, "The Georgia Peach"
3) Sal "The Barber" Maglie
12) Bill "Moose" Skowron
8) Harry "Suitcase" Simpson
2) Harold "Pie" Traynor
22) Rogers Hornsby, "The Rajah"
17) Harry "The Hat" Walker
9) Jim "Catfish" Hunter
14) Mark "The Bird" Fidrych
7) Stan "The Man" Musial
19) Joe "Ducky" Medwick
24) Dwight "Doc" Gooden
11) Harmon "Killer" Killebrew
23) Rich "Goose" Gossage
16) Greg "The Bull" Luzinski
10) George Herman "Babe" Ruth
4) Ken "The Hawk" Harrelson
13) Reggie Jackson, "Mr. October"
5) Roger "The Rocket" Clemens

Pitcher Sal Maglie was called The Barber because he'd give you a shave (and sometimes a haircut) if you crowded the plate. "Suitcase" Simpson got his moniker from his batting stance. Reggie Jackson earned the name Mr. October for his great post-season average. And Bob Uecker's nickname, Mr. Baseball, is sarcastic.

41. Mugs

1) Gertrude Stein
2) Leonard Bernstein
3) Artur Rubinstein
4) The Bride of Frankenstein
   (Elsa Lanchester)
5) Albert Einstein
6) Gloria Steinem
7) George Steinbrenner
8) John Steinbeck
9) Oscar Hammerstein II

42. Figures of speech

1) dirigible	13) intaglio
2) unruly	14) rigging
3) oddball	15) martyr
4) bribe (not bride or pride)	16) tariff
5) patio	17) katydid
6) putrid	18) turgid
7) intriguing	19) triumphant
8) quartz	20) gingiva
9) czarina	21) piquant
10) ecliptic	22) highfalutin
11) unhurt	23) mirth
12) buck (not puck, duck, quick or ouch)	24) mulatto

43. Board work

The four pieces hidden in the chessboard's troughs are the White King on Q3, the Black King on Q3, the Black Knight on KN6, and the Black Bishop on KN3.

Black's last move (N-KN6ch) proves that there's a Black Bishop at KN3, which checked White's King. White answers by capturing the attacking Bishop with the Knight at K5 (NxBch), thereby discovering a check against Black's King by the Bishop at B4. Black can forestall mate with P-K4, but not for long. White's BxP mates.

White	Black
. . .	N-KN6ch
NxBch	P-K4
BxP mate	

44. Old Test.

Hebrew, like Arabic, is written from right to left. The message, from Genesis 11:9, read:

Therefore is the
name of it called
Babel
because the Lord
did there confound
the language
of all the earth
and from thence
did the Lord
scatter them abroad
upon the face
of all the earth

אי קרקכסרק זד איק
משצק סכ זא בשרדקג
נשנקך
נקבש ודק איק לסרג
גזג איקרק בסמכסומג
איק רשמעושעק
סכ שרך איק קשראי
שמג כרסצ אי קמבק
גזג איק לסרג
דבשאאקר איקצ שנרסשג
רפסמ איק כשבק
סכ שרך איק קשראי

45. Locations

Banff?

The starry-eyed koala bear (7), kangaroo (11), Australian flag (12), and letter "A" (15) symbolize Australia; the six-pointed Star of David (14), Israel; the oriental-looking zoetrope (9), Tokyo; the letter "I" (1), Italy; the bird and Arabic script (3), Arabian Gulf States; the Canadian Rockies (2), Banff; the lion (5), Czechoslovakia; the Union Jack (10), England; the five-pointed stars (6) and "USA" (8), the United States; and the maple leaf (4) and letter "C" (13), Canada.

Banff is a city in Alberta, Canada. A zoetrope is a primitive animation device.

7,11,12,15	Australia
14	Israel
9	Tokyo
1	Italy
3	Arabian Gulf States
2	Banff
5	Czechoslovakia
10	England
6,8	United States
4,13	Canada

46. C-2?

a 9   (A-10 Thunderbolt II, USA)
b 11 (F-16 Fighting Falcon, USA)
c 1   (Lightning, UK)
d 8   (OV-10 Bronco, USA)
e 5   (F-104 Starfighter, USA)
f 7   (Fresco, USSR)
g 4   (OV-1 Mohawk, USA)
h 10 (Fitter, USSR)
i 3   (A-7 Corsair, USA)
j 6   (A-4 Skyhawk, USA)
k 2   (Buccaneer, UK)

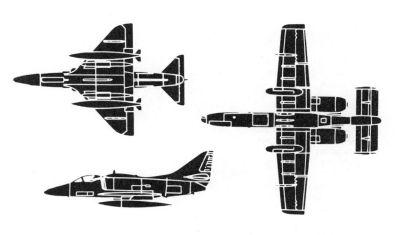

47. I-cues

The following answers were right between the i's:

Pepsi, Miami
airline (or airlift), dial
dirigible
Ritz (or HiHo), bingo, aim (or hit)
film, magnify (or examine)
Kiwanis, aspirin
insignia, sign
pipeline (or oilspill), mi ti (or hi fi)

48. Medicine chest

1)   Vaseline petroleum jelly
2)   Jergens lotion
3)   Mennen Skin Bracer
4)   Scope mouthwash
5)   Barbasol shaving cream
6)   Kaopectate
7)   Oil of Olay beauty cream
8)   Phillips' milk of magnesia
9)   Sucrets
10) Vaseline Intensive Care
11) Desenex foot spray
12) Sea & Ski suntan lotion
13) Johnson's Baby Powder
14) Arrid Extra Dry deodorant
15) Johnson's Baby Shampoo
16) Mennen Speed Stick deodorant
17) Chloraseptic
18) Tums antacid tablets
19) Right Guard deodorant
20) Selsun Blue dandruff shampoo
21) Vitalis (old label)
22) Crest toothpaste

49. Classic hits

Romantic Symphony — Bruckner
The Seasons — Haydn
Thus Spake Zarathustra — R. Strauss
Scenes from Childhood — Schumann
Die Fledermaus — J. Strauss
Oedipus Rex — Stravinsky
Symphonie fantastique — Berlioz
Organ Symphony — Saint-Saens
Ring of the Nibelungs — Wagner
Choral Symphony — Beethoven
Royal Fireworks Music — Handel
The Planets — Holst
Don Giovanni — Mozart

New World Symphony — Dvorak
Resurrection Symphony — Mahler
La Traviata — Verdi
Coffee Cantata — Bach
Peer Gynt — Grieg
Finlandia — Sibelius
Tales of Hoffmann — Offenbach
Funeral March Sonata — Chopin
Unfinished Symphony — Schubert
The Four Seasons — Vivaldi
La Boheme — Puccini
Scheherazade — Rimsky-Korsakov
Boris Godunov — Mussorgsky

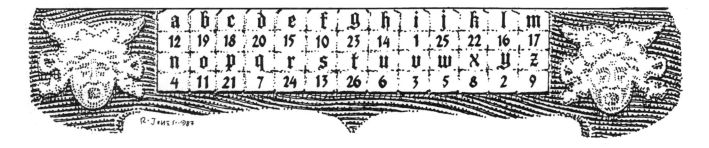

a	b	c	d	e	f	g	h	i	j	k	l	m
12	19	18	20	15	10	23	14	1	25	22	16	17

n	o	p	q	r	s	t	u	v	w	x	y	z
4	11	21	7	24	13	26	6	3	5	8	2	9

50. Silverwhere

1) Teaspoon
2) Table fork
3) Table knife
4) Tablespoon
5) Soup spoon
6) Salad fork
7) Lemon stick
8) Demitasse spoon
9) Long drink spoon
10) Nut spoon
11) Cheese knife
12) Cold meat fork
13) Pastry server
14) Melon spoon
15) Salad-serving fork
16) Sugar tongs
17) Carving fork
18) Carving knife
19) Table serving spoon
20) Table serving fork
21) Butter knife
22) Ice cream spoon
23) Soup ladle
24) Salt spoon
25) Salad-serving spoon
26) Punch ladle
27) Lobster fork
28) Snail tongs
29) Ice tongs
30) Spaghetti server

16   10   13   1   15   26   27   2   30   14   22   18   25   28   6

17   19   23   7   20   21   9   11   8   12   29   3   4   24   5

128